Advanced Issues in Property Valuation

Advanced Issues in Property Valuation

Hans Lind and Bo Nordlund

WILEY Blackwell

Registered Offices
John Wiley & Sons, Inc., 111 River Street, Hoboken, NJ 07030, USA
John Wiley & Sons Ltd, The Atrium, Southern Gate, Chichester, West Sussex, PO19 8SQ, UK

Editorial Office
9600 Garsington Road, Oxford, OX4 2DQ, UK

For details of our global editorial offices, customer services, and more information about Wiley products visit us at www.wiley.com.

Wiley also publishes its books in a variety of electronic formats and by print-on-demand. Some content that appears in standard print versions of this book may not be available in other formats.

Library of Congress Cataloging-in-Publication Data

Names: Lind, H. (Hans), author. | Nordlund, Bo, author.
Title: Advanced issues in property valuation : a textbook / Hans Lind, Bo Nordlund.
Description: Hoboken, NJ : Wiley-Blackwell, 2021.
Identifiers: LCCN 2021015372 (print) | LCCN 2021015373 (ebook) | ISBN 9781119783367 (paperback) | ISBN 9781119796220 (adobe pdf) | ISBN 9781119796244 (epub)
Subjects: LCSH: Real property–Valuation.
Classification: LCC HD1387 .L552 2021 (print) | LCC HD1387 (ebook) | DDC 333.33/2–dc23
LC record available at https://lccn.loc.gov/2021015372
LC ebook record available at https://lccn.loc.gov/2021015373

Cover Design: Wiley
Cover Image: Photographed by MR.ANUJAK JAIMOOK/Getty Images, Brzozowska/E+/Getty Images

Printed and bound by CPI Group (UK) Ltd, Croydon, CR0 4YY

C9781119783367_270421

Contents

Preface

As we have been working with issues related property valuation for many years, there is a large number of people who over the years have influenced our thinking and/or been part of projects that produced some of the research that this book is based on. We would especially like to mention Erik Persson, Stellan Lundström and Christina Gustafsson for many discussions on valuation issues. Neil Crosby is also a person that we have discussed many of these issues with over the years.

Christina Gustafsson should also be thanked for comments on an earlier version and especially the advice to relate the discussion more to documents produced by international organizations like Royal Institute of Chartered Surveyors (RICS) and the International Valuations Standards Council (IVSC). Four anonymous referees should also be thanked for constructive comments on an earlier version.

Finally, we would like to thank all the people at Wiley that have helped us in a constructive and efficient way.

Hans Lind
Bo Nordlund

1

Introduction

1.1 The General Purpose of the Book

There are a number of good basic textbooks on property valuation, e.g. *Property Valuation* by Peter Wyatt or the Appraisal Institute's classic book *The Appraisal of Real Estate*.[1] These books present basic concepts and valuation methods with a focus on what you need to know to work with valuation issues in the real estate sector, either as a producer of valuations or in a position where you use valuations, and need to understand and evaluate valuations.

This book has been written as a type of 'advanced' textbook that problematizes a number of issues that are presented in the basic textbooks. Things in reality are often not as clear as they are in the basic textbooks. There are different views of how useful different concepts and methods really are. Some of the controversies about concepts and methods typically arise in specific episodes on the market, e.g. after a crash on the market or in situations where there seem to be very optimistic views among actors in the market that may raise concerns whether e.g. real estate assets are 'overvalued' in the market. Other differences relate to differences between countries and local traditions. Even though there are international cooperation and standardization, such differences still remain. The aim of the book is to introduce readers to these discussions and to make it possible to have well-informed opinions on these issues. Some advanced textbooks focus on valuation of specific types of properties – from agriculture to hotels or special purpose buildings – but in this book, the focus is on what could be called more theoretical or conceptual issues, but also on some normative issues related to governance and the role of the valuer.

---

1 The list could be made longer and include e.g. Havard (2002), Baum and Crosby (2008), Scarrett and Osborn (2014) and Morri and Benedetto (2019).

Advanced Issues in Property Valuation, First Edition. Hans Lind and Bo Nordlund.

We think that there are at least two different audiences for the book. The first is students in courses on the Master level, where the student has already read one basic course in valuation or in larger basic courses, where the book can be used in the later part of the course. The book should also be useful in other academic courses, e.g. doctoral courses in real estate.

In an economy that changes quickly, there is also a need for courses for real estate practitioners who want to update and deepen their knowledge about property valuation. We have met the opinion that practitioners primarily want 'cookbooks' that tell them exactly what to do and that their interest in more conceptual and theoretical issues is limited. As teachers in a large number of such courses, we strongly disagree. In our view, almost everybody wants to understand what they are doing, why things are done in a certain way and alternative ways of looking at things. A broader perspective should also increase creativity and problem-solving ability for practioners.

1.2 Overview of Issues Covered

The central concept of market value is discussed in Chapter 2. There are several issues that have been discussed concerning market value. Should the definition refer to prudent and knowledgeable actors when actors in the market are not always knowledgeable or prudent? Conditions that a good definition should fulfil are also discussed in this chapter. The connection between price and turnover also creates problems as observed prices alone then do not reflect the situation on the market. Problems with the concept of highest and best use are also discussed.

Other value concepts than market value are discussed in Chapter 5 that covers valuation for lending purposes, and in Chapter 6 about valuation in accounting contexts.

Chapter 3 looks closer at valuation methods. Typically, these are divided into sales comparisons, income and cost methods (or approaches), but what is really the logic behind this division? It is argued that some of the methods that are often called income methods really should be classified as sales comparison methods. A new classification of valuation is sketched. As properties are heterogenous, there are almost always a need to make adjustments for the remaining differences between the property to be valued and the objects compared with. Different such adjustment methods are also described. Finally, two more general issues are discussed in this chapter: Why is regression analysis not used more in property valuation and how can discounted cash flow methods lead to a market value?

Uncertainty and bias in property valuations often come to the fore in discussion about property valuations after a downturn in the market. The old, high valuations are questioned by investors that have lost money, and there is a demand for more discussions about uncertainties in valuations. In Chapter 4, different interpretations of uncertainty and bias are discussed, e.g. that valuers disagree or that observed prices differ from estimated market value. Possible bias caused by client pressure and the stability of the value are also covered together with possible recommendations to improve the quality of valuation from the perspective of giving the reader an idea about how uncertain the estimated market value is.

Chapter 5 analyses valuation for lending purposes and long-term value concepts. A crucial issue in this context is the predictability of market prices and if price bubbles can be identified in advance. Can the risk for falling prices be handled by adjusting the Loan-to-Value ratio or do we need other value concepts than (current) market value? Mortgage lending value and worth are examples of such concepts. The most general question covered is, if rules about valuation can reduce the risk for future real estate-related crises?

Valuation for accounting purposes and other accounting-related issues are covered in Chapter 6. The fair value concept and its relation to market value is discussed together with the concepts entry price and exit price and especially how fair value should be interpreted in thin markets. The fair value hierarchy concerning valuation methods is discussed both in this chapter and in Chapter 3. There is also a section about quality in financial reporting.

Sustainability and property valuation is discussed in Chapter 7. What is really meant by a sustainable building and what should we expect to be the difference in value between 'brown' and 'green' buildings? Are special methods needed for valuing sustainable buildings? What should we expect to happen with the value difference over time?

Chapter 8 is about transparency and property markets. Transparency is an important topic both for the real estate market as such and for the valuation process as reported in valuation reports. It is, however, underlined that there are limits to transparency in both these areas. Having more information than others is something that can lead to higher profits, both for real estate investors and for valuation companies. As property valuers also use experience and a 'feeling about' where the market is going, it is hard to make the valuation process completely transparent.

Ethics, the role of the valuer and governance are covered in Chapter 9. Not least because of climate change and other sustainability issues, it is more and more expected that all companies and professional groups take a broader perspective on their activities. Companies formulate sustainability policies and policies about corporate social responsibility (CSR). On the other hand, it is questionable to what extent valuers can 'lead' the market. Important issues are also the credibility of valuers and problems caused by asymmetric information including problems for buyers to evaluate the quality of a valuation product. Authorization or certification systems are discussed as one way to reduce these problems.

In Chapter 10, three issues are covered. The first is technological development, e.g. in the form of artificial intelligence systems. The second is possible structural changes caused by unexpected events, illustrated by the corona-pandemic. The third issue discussed is ideas about 'radical uncertainty' and what that might imply for property valuations.

1.3 How the Book Can be Used

Most chapters start with an overview of what is said in basic textbooks, and then discussions from scientific articles are added. In each chapter, central articles are referred to. New articles are continuously published, and it is important that teachers try to update course materials in relation to recent ideas and arguments. Such an update can also be made as student exercises, where students are given the task to find more recent articles and then relate what they find in these texts to what is said in the book.

Knowing local conditions (in a country or region) is always important for students as this is the market where most of them will work in the future. In each chapter, there are a number of specific exercises that can be used in courses. Many of these are of the type 'Interview local actors about how they look at XX' or 'Interview local actors about current problems and controversies about XX'.

Many of the issues discussed are multidimensional and it is not easy to evaluate all aspects and take a stand on the issues. One format that we have found useful and popular among students is 'Pro and con debates'. In many chapters, there are suggestions about topics for such debates. Students are then divided into teams and should make a presentation arguing either for or against a specific proposition. In a second round, they should present counterarguments to the arguments presented by the opposing team, etc.

2

The Concept of Market Value

2.1 Introduction

There are two fundamental value concepts: Market value and Investment value or Worth (IVSC 2019, p. 17). Investment value is a rather uncomplicated concept as it simply refers to the value from a specific owner's/investor's perspective. This is calculated by a standard investment analysis in the form of a cash-flow analysis. The inputs are then expected net operating income from that actor's perspective and the rate of return this actor demands and the expected residual value at the end of this actor's expected holding period. Such a residual value is normally calculated from the expected net operating income at the end of the calculation/holding period.

Market value is important in a number of different contexts, e.g. when transactions are made, when property is used as collateral for lending and in financial reports. The fact that this value concept is so important, and as will be clear below, rather complicated, it is important to look closer at the definition of this concept. A number of aspects will be covered in this chapter, but value concepts will also be discussed in Chapter 5, and in Chapter 6. In Chapter 6 the concept of Fair value and its relation to market value will be discussed. It could also be useful to be aware of the distinctions between entry price and exit price explained in that chapter, where entry price at the date of a transaction is what has been paid and exit price what could be fetched if the property is sold at that date.

There are also other economic (value) concepts than market value and investment value that may be relevant in different situations. Examples of such value concepts are acquisition cost/-value, replacement cost/-value or long-term values of different kinds. We will further discuss such value concepts in Chapters 5 and 6.

Advanced Issues in Property Valuation, First Edition. Hans Lind and Bo Nordlund.
© 2021 John Wiley & Sons Ltd. Published 2021 by John Wiley & Sons Ltd.

2.2 Standard Definition

The International Valuation Standards defines market value as follows (IVSC 2019, p. 18):

> Market value is the estimated amount for which an asset or liability should exchange on the valuation date between a willing buyer and a willing seller in an arm's length transaction after proper marketing where the parties had each acted knowledgeably, prudently, and without compulsion.

This definition is also the official one in the United Kingdom and accepted by RICS. In the RICS Valuation – Global standards (RICS 2019), the standards from IVSC are included in full as Part 6 of that book.

The US Appraisal Institute presents the following definition (Appraisal Institute 2013, p. 58):

> The most probable price, as of a specified date, in cash or in terms equivalent to cash, or in other precisely revealed terms, for which the specified property rights should sell after reasonable exposure in a competitive market under all conditions requisite to a fair sale, with the buyer and seller each acting prudently, knowledgably, and for self-interest, and assuming that neither is under undue duress.

Looking closer at these definitions, some common elements can be found:

- A date of valuation (a measurement date).
- Reference to the amount that the property should exchange for after proper marketing (reasonable exposure, in an orderly transaction).
- Reference to buyers and sellers acting knowledgably and prudently: this is discussed in Section 2.4.
- Reference to a willing buyer/willing seller: this is discussed in Section 2.5.

But there are also some differences:

- The IVSC/RICS definition refers to 'the *estimated* amount' while the US definition refers to 'the *most probable* price' (discussed in Section 2.4).
- The US definition refers to 'a competitive market' but there is no such reference in the IVSC one: this is discussed in Section 2.6).

Another problem that will be discussed in this chapter is the relation between turnover and market price, and whether turnover in some way should be included in the definition (Section 2.8). In both the standards, there is also a discussion about 'highest and best use' and this will be discussed in Section 2.9.

2.3   Criteria for a Good Definition: Clear, Measurable, Concise and Relevant

The point of making a definition is to clarify a concept and therefore the words used in the definition must be *clear in the sense that they are interpreted and applied in a similar way by different actors.*[1] If a word is vague, there might be disagreement about whether it is correct to apply it in a specific situation. Additional explanations may sometimes be needed to make sure that the readers will apply the term in the same way and such clarifications can, for example, be found in IVSC (2019, pp. 18–20).

A second criterion for a good definition is that it *refers to things that are measurable*, at least in principle. If valuers disagree, it should at least in a number of circumstances be possible to find data that indicate which estimate is closer to the truth. RICS (2019, p. 2) states that 'Consistency, objectivity and transparency are fundamental to building and sustaining public confidence and trust in valuation'. Objectivity in the context of a definition could be interpreted as that there exist data/evidence that substantiate at least a claim that the market value is closer to A than to B.

A definition should also be *concise and not include terms that do not add any further content* to the definition. This condition is sometimes referred to as Occam's razor, i.e. unnecessary components in the definition should deleted.

The final condition for a good definition of market value is that the definition should lead to a concept that is *relevant in the context where the term normally is used.* A definition of market value should be such that market value - so defined - will be of interest for potential buyers and sellers thinking about a future transaction, or for measuring the wealth of a company in the balance sheet.

2.4   Problem 1: 'Estimated Price' or 'Most Probable Price'?

As there always are uncertainty about the price that is possible to fetch when selling a specific property at a specific point in time, the formulation 'most probable price' seems to be the best as this uncertainty then is clear. In IVSC (2019, p. 18), 'the estimated amount' is also explained in terms of 'the most probable price reasonably obtainable in the market', even though it is not clear what 'reasonably obtainable' adds to the formulation.

This does not, however, solve all problems. Suppose that there are 10 observations from recent transactions of very similar properties. Should the most probable price refer to the mean value or to the median value? If the observations

---

1 See Lind (1998) for a discussion about these criteria.

are skewed, there can be rather large differences between the mean and the median. As valuers usually are suspicious against 'outliers', the median should perhaps be the most relevant concept.

The next question is how 'most probable' should be interpreted in the context of property valuation. As discussed in Lind (1998), there are at least two definitions of probability, or two different ways of looking at the concept of probability.

The first is the *frequency interpretation* of probability. In this interpretation, saying, for example, that the probability is 1/6 to get the number 3 when throwing a dice would simply mean that if the dice is thrown a large number of times, then the result would be a number 3 in 1/6 of the throws.

This interpretation is, however, rather meaningless in a real estate valuation context as it is not practically possible to sell the same property a large number of times during a short period of time. Even in a rather homogenous market, there is a limited number of transactions. Defining the most probable price as the average of the observed prices would be the same as saying that the probability of getting a number 3 is not 1/6 because the frequency of getting number 3 differed from 1/6 in the first 10 throws. With a frequency interpretation of probability, it would therefore not be possible to present convincing evidence whether a certain price is the most probable or not.

A second interpretation of probability is the *logical interpretation,* where probability measures the degree of confidence that is rationally justified by the available evidence. This interpretation seems very suitable in a property valuation context. When a valuer, for example, asserts that the value is 100, it would in this interpretation mean that given the available evidence it is more rational to believe in a price around 100 than to believe in a price around 90 or around 110. Controversies about the value of a specific property can also typically be seen as controversies about the interpretation of the relevant evidence. A valuation method is from this perspective a method to collect and analyse evidence in order to arrive at rational belief about what the price will be if the property is sold.

The conclusion in this section is then that the formulation 'most probable price' is the best one and that it can be explained further by saying that it refers to the price for which there is the strongest arguments, or for which there is the strongest evidence.

2.5 Problem 2: Shall the Definition Refer to a Competitive Market?

A special feature of the Appraisal Institute definition is that it refers to the price in 'a competitive market', while there is no such reference in the IVSC definition.

Here, we would side with the IVSC definition, primarily with reference to the criteria that a good definition should be relevant for actors on the market. Actual property markets differ in size and in the number of actors on the market and can be evaluated as more or less competitive. Independently of the level of competition, actors can be expected to be interested in the probable price if a property is to be sold or bought. The conclusion must then be that market value should be defined in such a way that it is applicable independently of how competitive the specific market is. It should be possible to discuss the market value of a unique property and of a property on a thin market, and this means that a reference to 'a competitive market' should not be included in the definition of market value.

Including such a condition would also create methodological problems. If market value is defined as the probable price on a competitive market and the current market is not so competitive, there is no observable evidence about the price on the competitive market. Observed prices could not be used directly to make inferences about the market value and that is a big problem as valuation should be based on observable evidence.

2.6 Problem 3: Should the Definition Refer to Prudent and Knowledgeable Actors?

The condition that parties had acted knowledgeably and prudently is clarified in the following way in IVSC (2019, p. 19–20):

> presumed that both the willing buyer and the willing seller are reasonably informed about the nature and characteristics of the asset, its actual and potential uses, and the state of the market as the valuation date. . . . the prudent buyer or seller will act in accordance with the best market information available at the time.

There are two problems with including this kind of formulation. First, it raises empirical problems. What is the state of the market? What is the best market information at that time? How can the valuers *know* what is the best market information available – and what it means to act in accordance with this information? Some actors in the market rely on intuition and gut-feeling, and is such behaviour inconsistent with being prudent? And if comparative sales are used during the valuation process, how should the valuer find out whether these sales fulfil the conditions that the parties had acted prudently and knowledgeable? We would suggest that there can be large differences in opinion about those issues, both among actors in the market, valuers and followers of the market, especially during boom periods. Robert Shiller argued in a famous book (Shiller 2000) that share prices in the late 1990s was based on 'irrational exuberance'. Some would probably say the same about the property market in many countries during the late 1980s or during the period before the financial crises around 2009. If transactions were carried out by people with 'irrational exuberance', those transactions would not be relevant for evaluating the market value at that point in time – if the market value is defined as the expected price given knowledgeable actors. Some of the problems that this leads to will be discussed also in Chapter 5 when the concept mortgage lending value is discussed.

The second argument against including reference to prudent and knowledge actors is the same as the argument against including a reference to competitive markets. In reality, the prudence and knowledge differ between actors, between markets and over time, and the market value concept should be applicable independently of the characteristics of the actors on the market. Adding references to prudence and knowledge reduces the relevance of the market value so defined, especially when a valuation is done for transaction purposes.

The conclusion would therefore be that the conditions about prudence and knowledgeability should not be included in the definition. The valuer should look at the current market as it is and should not have to evaluate whether the actors in this market are rational or not, given a certain interpretation of rationality. It should also be remembered that the market value definition refers to the most probable price, and if there now and then are (especially) stupid actors on the market – paying too much or selling to cheap compared to other transactions at the same time – those prices would simply not be rational to expect and should therefore not be given great weight when the market value is estimated. This means that the valuer might need to evaluate what lies behind certain transactions with deviating prices, but there is no need to evaluate whether the actors on the market in general are acting prudently or knowledgably.

2.7 Problem 4: Should the Definition Include a Reference to Willing Seller and Willing Buyer?

The interpretation of the condition about *willing seller* can be very important – and problematic. The alternative to including this condition is to define market value explicitly as the most probable price *if* a property is put on the market. In such an interpretation, it is completely irrelevant whether this is a price that the current owner would be willing to sell the property for.

If the condition about willing seller is taken seriously, the following situation could occur. Assume that the maximum price anyone is willing to pay for a property is 100, and that there are several actors who are willing to pay 100. None of the current owners are, however, willing to sell at that price as they think it is too low and that prices soon will increase. There are therefore no transactions on the market. If the condition about willing seller is not included in the definition, the conclusion would be that the market value is 100. If the condition of willing seller is included in the definition, the conclusion should be that there is no market value - as there is no price that buyers and sellers could agree on.

IVSC (2019, p. 19) makes the following clarification: 'The willing seller is motivated to sell the asset at market terms for the best price attainable in the open market after proper marketing, whatever that price may be'. But this means that the inclusion of the condition of a willing seller does not add anything to the definition and should therefore be deleted. However, it is important to bear in mind that there could be transactions on the market that can be called 'forced sales' that may not be representative when analysing comparable sales to include as basis in a market valuation. We will discuss the concept of 'forced sales' later in this section.

The conclusion so far would then be that market value should be interpreted as the probable price in the hypothetical situation where the property is put on the market given the current conditions, independently of the views of the current owner. This interpretation has consequences especially for valuation for balance sheet purposes which will be returned to in Chapter 6.

The condition of *willing buyer* also seems either problematic or redundant. All definitions refer to transactions on a market and it is implicit in this formulation that the probable price refers to a normal transaction where no buyer is forced to sign the contract. The conclusion would then be that Occam's razor can be used to delete both the conditions about willing buyer and willing seller. IVSC (2019, p. 19) makes the following clarification: 'The buyer is . . . one who purchase in accordance with the realities of the current market and with current market expectations . . .. The assumed buyer would not pay a higher price than the market requires'. This, however, creates a number of problems: How can the valuer know 'the realities of the current market' and 'the price that the market requires'? Should we not expect that there are disagreements about what these realities and expectations are, and that this would lead to disagreements about what sales to include in a comparative sales analysis? These problems would be avoided by simply deleting the condition about a willing buyer.

A market value should not be mixed up with a 'forced sales' value. A forced sale could end up with a lower price than what could have been expected because of limited time to expose the property on the market. Therefore, transactions classified as forced sales may not be appropriate to use as comparable sales. However, a valuer should also take the following into account when evaluating whether a transaction should be regarded as forced or not (see IVSC 2019, p. 26):

> Sales in an inactive or falling market are not automatically 'forced sales' simply because a seller might hope for a better price if conditions improved. Unless the seller is compelled to sell by a deadline that prevents proper marketing, the seller will be a willing seller within the definition of Market Value
>
> *(see IVSC 2019, paras 30.1–30.7).*

2.8 Problem 5: Market Value and Turnover

There are no references to turnover in either of the definitions of market value presented in the beginning of this chapter. The most probable explanation for this is that the definitions assume that there is a considerable number of potential buyers that are willing to buy a property for roughly the same price, e.g. on an active housing market with many similar properties. In such a situation, the demand curve is almost horizontal in a rather large interval on the quantity-axis. A consequence of this is that changes in turnover will not have a strong effect on the price. This is illustrated in Figure 2.1.

But how realistic is really this assumption? In the commercial real estate market, possible buyers may have rather different views on the potential of a property and the future development of the market where the property is located. On the residential market, actors might differ in preferences, in their incomes and in their expectations about the future development of the market. In both cases, the reservation prices of the actors on the market might differ considerably. Differences in knowledge may also lead to differences in reservation prices. The effect of these differences in reservation prices is that there will be a downward sloping demand curve, and that the expected price – the market value - will depend on the number of properties that are put on the market during a certain period of time. However, it is also important to bear in mind that the market value concept in itself is independent of the numbers of transactions in the market. If there is a small number of transactions, or maybe no transactions at all, the aim when estimating market value is still to find a hypothetical price in a transaction on market terms at the value date. (We will discuss issues connected to valuation methods that may be applied in thin markets more in detail in Chapter 3, and especially in the context of so-called 'actor-based methods'.)

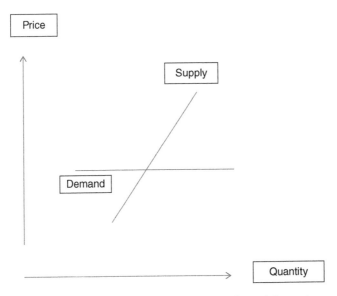

Figure 2.1 Price and quantity with an almost horizontal demand curve.

Haurin (2005) discusses changes in liquidity/turnover in the context of creating a real estate price index. The variation in turnover during the business cycle will smooth prices, as prices will not rise so much when more properties are put on the market during the boom, and not fall so much when turnover goes down during a recession. An extreme case is illustrated in Figure 2.2, where no property owner is willing to sell at a price below the current one. The supply curve is then horizontal at the current price up to the current level of turnover. A fall in demand will in such a situation lead to a fall in turnover, but the observed prices will not fall. It has been argued that this is actually what happened in Sweden when the financial crisis hit the real estate market in the fall of 2008. The current owners were financially stable and did not sell when demand fell. The market died and there were almost no transactions and no new prices were observed on the market, which created problems for valuers.

A low interest rate can make these fluctuations in turnover stronger. The low interest rate can make it easier to hold out when there is a downturn in demand as debt costs fall. A low interest rate also makes it less costly to wait and therefore the expected future prices do not have to be so much higher than the current price in order to make it rational to wait. Assume that the current market value – in the recession – is 100. If the rate of return demanded is 10%, then it is rational to wait if the price in a year is expected to be higher than 110. But if the rate of return

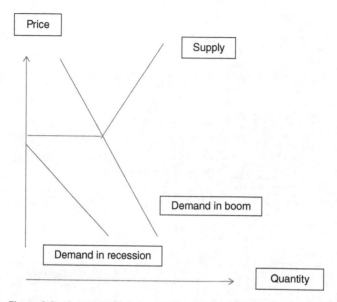

Figure 2.2 Price and quantity with a partly horizontal supply curve.

demanded is 4%, then it is rational to wait if the price in a year is expected to be higher than 104.

The underlying 'problem' is that transactions are voluntary and that the willingness to buy and sell depends on market conditions. Observed transactions are not the result of a random selection of properties that is put on the market. Given the economic conditions, institutional structure and the beliefs of the actors, a certain change in demand can lead to very different reactions on the market: In some cases, transaction volumes fall much and prices only a little, while in other cases, observed prices fall much but turnover only a little. The development during the financial crisis 2008 can illustrate this where observed prices for commercial property hardly fell at all in Sweden while they fell much and quickly in England (see Crosby et al. 2010) – even though the underlying fall in GDP was roughly the same.

It might not be necessary to make assumptions about turnover explicit in the definition of market value, but it could be an advantage to add a clause saying 'given expected turnover' in the definition. The relation between turnover and price, when there is a downward sloping demand curve, will, however, affect uncertainty in the estimation of market value. This will be returned to both in Chapter 4 on uncertainty and in Chapter 6, where we discuss exit prices in thin markets in the context of valuation for financial reports.

2.9   Highest and Best Use

Both IVSC (2019) and Appraisal Institute (2013) use the concept of 'Highest and best use'. IVSC (2019, p. 25) writes, 'The market value of an asset will reflect its highest and best use' and this is explained in terms of the use that maximizes its potential (given what is possible, legally permissible and financially feasible). Similar formulations can be found in Appraisal Institute (2013, p. 42).

There are problems with this concept and our recommendation is that it should be used with a great degree of caution when market value is discussed. The requirements for empirically extracted 'evidence' should be high if, or when, this concept is claimed to have affected an estimated market value-figure. As will be returned to in Chapter 8, the typical situation in a market is that actors have different knowledge, different expectations and different plans for a specific property. One actor may see possibilities that other actors initially are not aware of. An example discussed in Chapter 7 is that one investor sees that a certain building can be made green with a rather small investment. More theoretically, this can be described in terms of different views on the real options that a property has. In a market, actors typically gain by not giving away information and not telling others what their plans are. Investors may have plans that valuers are not aware of. If only one actor is aware of certain profitable opportunities that 'highest and best use' will not affect the bids of others are therefore not the price if the property is sold by a standard English auction, where bids are presented in ascending order until there is only one bidder left.

In a world of uncertainty, expectations are very important for what an actor is willing to pay. This means that even if a majority of investors and valuers believe that use A is the highest and best use, a very optimistic actor that believes that B is the highest and best might be willing to pay more.

These arguments imply that it may be questionable to say that the market price reflects the highest and best use, and the formulation does not add anything to the definitions discussed above. But it is very important to think about options when valuing a property and how this can be done is discussed in the next chapter.

2.10   Conclusion

Different countries have somewhat different definitions of market value, and valuers in the specific market have to follow the local practice in the interpretation of market value. The arguments above concerning clarity, conciseness and relevance, however, point in the direction of a simpler definition. The market value could be defined as

The most probable price, as of a specified date, in an arm's-length transaction after proper marketing given current market conditions and the expected level of turnover.

Even if this proposed definition differs somewhat from the official IVSC and US definitions above, our belief is that valuers in practice actually follow this shorter definition. They estimate a market value on a property given current market conditions even if the competitiveness on the market is rather low. They do not investigate how rational buyers and sellers have been in earlier transaction, unless there have been extreme conditions of some kind. But if there have been extreme conditions in a certain transaction, such a transaction should in any case be given little weight when the market value is estimated as the definition refers to the most probable price.

Exercises

1 What value concepts are used in your local market? Is there any differences between the local definitions and the one in IVSC? How do local valuers look at conditions related to knowledgeable actors?

2 Company A just won a 'closed' bidding contest and acquired an investment property for 135 Cash Units (CU). However, after the acquisition, it was found out that other bids on the property was 100 CU, 98 CU, 101 CU, 99 CU, 96 CU and lower. Two weeks after the acquisition, Company A has to present an estimation of market value (could be, for example, for lending or financial reporting purposes). Can Company A claim 135 as a market value? If not, why?

3

Finding the Market Value: What Is a Valuation Method and How Should the Methods Be Categorized?

3.1 Introduction and Overview

The chapter starts with a discussion of the three classic valuation methods or approaches: market or sales comparison method, income method and cost method. They are only discussed from the perspective of finding the market value of a property. We compare how they are described in some basic textbooks and in valuation standards, and point out some problems, especially how to draw the line between the sales comparison approach and other approaches. This problem is described more in detail in Section 3.3, and it points to the need for a more fundamental discussion about what can be called the information base of valuation (Section 3.4).

In Section 3.5, the result from these discussions is used to sketch an alternative classification based on how the link to the market is accomplished. Three basic approaches are presented: A sales comparison approach, an actor-based approach – where the link to the market is through knowledge of how actors in the market think and reason – and an approach where the valuer uses information from the stock market.

Independently of which approach/method is used, there will always be a need to make adjustment to take into account special characteristics of the property to be valued. Different methods to make such adjustments are discussed in Section 3.6. Sections 3.7–3.9 cover some more specific issues: the first is why statistical regression analysis of price data has not replaced the standard valuation methods (3.7), how a cash-flow analysis really can lead to a market value (3.8), valuation of development properties (3.9) and the use of several methods to estimate a market value (3.10).

French and Gabrielli (2018) make a distinction between approaches, methods and models. The three traditional approaches are mentioned (income, cost and market), but there is no explicit definition of an approach. A method is defined as 'an overall structure for the valuation' and a model as the 'detailed application of a mathematical technique' (p. 394). We think that such a terminology could create more confusion as people cannot be expected to remember and use terms like method and model in the same way. Our recommendation is therefore to using method and approach as synonyms and not make any distinction between them. Then, one can discuss variants within a method/approach and variants within these variants, but no new terminology is needed for that.

3.2   The Three Classic Valuation Approaches/Methods

3.2.1   The Sales Comparison Approach

In the US-textbook *The Appraisal of Real Estate* (2013), it is written (p. 36):

> In the sales comparison approach, value is indicated by recent sales of comparable properties in the market.

Later, they give a somewhat broader definition (p. 377):

> In the sales comparison approach, the appraiser develops an opinion of value by analyzing closed sales, listings, or pending sales of properties that are similar to the subject property.

The observed price can be related to different 'units of comparison' and these are exemplified (p. 386) by price per square meter, price per apartment unit and price per guest room for hotels. They, however, also give 'total revenue multiplier' as an example of a unit of comparison when valuing Golf courses with the sales comparison approach.

In Wyatt (2013), 'the comparison method' is simply described as follows:

> A property may be valued by comparing to similar properties for which recent price information is available. (p. 103).

In IVSC (2019) and RICS (2019), 'the market approach' is defined as follows:

> The market approach provides an indication of value by comparing the asset with identical or comparable (that is similar) assets for which price information is available. (p. 30)

They also note that the market approach uses various multipliers or units of comparison and exemplifies this with price per square meter and capitalization rates (p. 32). All multipliers are, however, not seen as being part of the market approach:

> Even in circumstances where the market approach is not used, the use of market-based inputs should be maximised in the application of other approaches (e.g., market-based valuation metrics such as effective yields and rates of return) (p. 32)

3.2.2 The Income Approach

In 'The Appraisal of Real Estate', the income approach is described as follows:

> The income capitalization approach to value consists of methods, techniques, and mathematical procedures that an appraiser uses to analyze a property's capacity to generate benefits (i.e., usually the monetary benefits of income and reversion) and convert these benefits into an indication of present value. (p. 439)

The income approach covers both 'direct capitalization' and cash-flow methods explained as follows:

> Direct capitalization is a method used in the income capitalization approach to convert a single year's income expectancy into a value indication. This conversion is accomplished in one step, by dividing the net operating income estimate by an appropriate income rate. (p. 491)
>
> Discounted cash flow (DCF) analysis is an appropriate tool for valuing any pattern of regular or irregular income. In many markets and for many property types, DCF analysis is the technique that investors prefer. The proper application of DCF analysis identifies the market conditions investors are anticipating as of the date of value. (p. 529)

These two versions are described as the implicit and the explicit model in French and Sloane (2018).

Wyatt (2013) also describes two different versions of the income approach. The first is the Investment method: 'methods of capitalizing rental income as a means of pricing property investments' (p. 114). As in the Appraisal of Real Estate, this includes both direct capitalization of (adjusted) net operating income (NOI) and cash-flow methods taking a longer period into account. The second version described is the *Profits method* (for properties that are inextricably linked to the business that operate from them): 'these premises are valued by capitalising their estimated future trading potential (as opposed to capitalising their estimated rental income)'.[1]

IVSC (2019) presents the following definition:

> Although there are many ways to implement the income approach, methods under the income approach are effectively based on discounting future amounts of cash flow to present value. They are variations of the Discounted Cash Flow (DCF) method. (p. 37)

This seems to be a somewhat narrower definition, as it only includes versions of the discounted cash-flow method. Both Wyatt and the Appraisal Institute include direct capitalization methods as part of the income approach and not only discounted cash flow or similar methods. IVSC seems to classify direct capitalization as a market approach, and this will be discussed further in Section 3.3.

In several textbooks, one can find very detailed descriptions of how the income method can be used, e.g. in Havard (2002) and Baum and Crosby (2008), especially for valuation of properties with different structures of the income stream.

3.2.3 The Cost Approach

In the Appraisal of Real Estate, 'The cost approach' is defined as follows:

> In the cost approach, a property is valued based on a comparison with the cost to build a new or substitute property. The cost estimate is adjusted for the depreciation evident in the existing property. (p. 562)

Wyatt (p. 171) writes about 'the replacement cost method' and that:

> This method is based on ...that a potential buyer would pay no more for the subject property than the cost of acquiring an equivalent new one .... the cost of an equivalent new one must be written down or depreciated to reflect differences between it and the subject property being valued. (p. 171)

IVSC (2019) writes in a way that is similar to Wyatt:

> The cost approach provides an indication of value using the economic principle that a buyer will pay no more for an asset than the cost to obtain an asset of equal utility, whether by purchase or by construction, unless undue

---

1 The related concept of Business Enterprise Value is discussed in the appendix.

time, inconvenience, risk or other factors are involved. The approach provides an indication of value by calculating the current replacement or reproduction cost of an asset and making deductions for physical deterioration and all other relevant forms of obsolescence (p. 44).

In this book, the cost approach is only looked upon as a method to reach a market value. It should, however, be remembered that the approach typically is used to determine other value concepts, like the cost-based depreciated replacement cost. For a building that a company has constructed, this can be classified as an entry price while market value (or fair value in financial reporting) is an exit price.

The point of the comments above is that in some situations the cost of construction can give valuable information concerning at least that the market value cannot be (considerably) higher than the cost of production, e.g. if it is a new property where it is easy for actors on the market to produce new similar units. As will be returned to below, there might also – in some markets in some time periods - be an observable relation between cost and price, and then cost can be an 'unit of comparison' in a sales comparison approach.

Regarding the cost approach and the replacement cost method, the following statement in Wyatt (2009) should be noted:

> Defining replacement cost as a method of estimating market value rather than a separate basis of value blurs the distinction between cost and value. This paper argues that market value assumptions do not hold in the case of the replacement cost method.

A hypothesis could be that cost-based methods could work well in stable markets where there is a fixed quota between entry price (here, e.g. the construction cost) and exit price (here the market value). This quota should, however, normally be derived from observed transactions.

3.2.4 Are There Other Approaches?

In all classifications, there are borderline cases or cases where different methods are integrated. A good example is what Wyatt (2013, p. 187) calls the Residual Method. This is used for valuing development properties and uses both market data and cost data. Market data are used to estimate the value of the property when the building is ready, and the value of the undeveloped land is estimated as the difference between that value and the cost of developing the property (see Section 3.9).

3.3 A Problem with the Standard Classifications

The sales comparison or market approach is the natural starting point when trying to estimate the market value, because looking at prices in recent transaction seems logical if the current probable price should be estimated.

A general problem with using the sales comparison approach, especially for commercial buildings, is that there always, or at least in most situations, are rather large differences between properties. The challenge for the valuer using the sales comparison approach is then to find a stable empirical relation between observed price and some observable characteristics of the property, i.e. use some kind of *normalization* of the observed prices. This is called a unit of comparison in the quotations above. There can, for example, be a stable relation between price and

- The area of the property. The *price paid per square meter* is then calculated from the observed sales, and this price per square meter is then used to estimate the most probably price of the property to be valued.
- The current rent level of the property. The *gross income multiplier* (price/rent ratio) might be stable in the observed transactions and can then be used to estimate the market value.
- The current NOI (rent minus operating costs). The *direct yield* (net operating income/price ratio) might be stable in the observed transactions and can then be used to estimate the market value.
- The cost of construction. In a stable competitive market, there should – as mentioned above - be a relation between *cost of construction and value*, even though it should be necessary to add age as a second determinant. A builder would not add costly features to a project unless these features are expected to increase the market value of the property. The differences in value between projects with different qualities should therefore be related to the cost of transforming these characteristics. The variable Tobin's Q – defined as the relation between price and cost of construction – might therefore in some cases be useful for predicting the probable price of a property.

It should be underlined that whether any of the quotas mentioned above are stable and suitable for determining the market value is a *purely empirical matter*. Any stable empirical relation between price and observable characteristics of the property can be used to estimate the probable price of a property with known observable characteristics.

The list of possible units of comparison above is not complete. For example, in Sweden, observed prices are sometimes related to the *assessed value for tax purposes* and if there is a stable relation between assessed value at time t-x and observed prices at t, this quota can be used to estimate the probable price for a property at time t. There is of course also room for innovations concerning characteristics that can be used to predict the price of property.

Different ways to normalize observed prizes could be called different *variants* of the sales comparison method. (In the terminology in French and Gabrielli (2018), they would be called different *methods* within a sales comparison *approach*.)

The implication of this discussion is that *some of the methods that in the literature above are classified as income or cost-based methods should correctly be classified as version of the sales comparison or market approach.* This is especially clear for the income methods, e.g. using the gross income multiplier and/or the direct yield (net capitalization) for estimating market value. In all these cases, the starting point is observed prices that then are normalized in one way or another in order to be useful for estimating the market value for a property in a market with heterogenous objects. Cost and income (gross or net) are then simply variables that can be the unit of comparison for the observed prices to make them useful for drawing conclusion about the probable price for the property that is to be valued. *Such methods should then be seen as versions of the sales comparison approach and not as a separate method or approach.* This is argued in detail in Lind and Nordlund (2014) and the idea that gross income multiplier and net capitalization are variants of the sales comparison approach and not an income approach is taken up in Morri and Benedetto (2019, p. 47f). They use the term 'direct comparison approach' independently of what unit of comparison is used, which means that direct capitalization of (normalized) NOI is seen as a sales comparison approach.

It is from this perspective interesting to note that in IVSC (2019), only the cash-flow method is mentioned as an income method. Capitalization rates are explicitly mentioned as a unit of comparison under the market approach. Even if it is not completely clear, they seem to have made adjustments in the description of the method to avoid the unclear boundary between sales comparison and income methods in the traditional classification.

3.4 The Information Base of a Valuation

In order to arrive at a clearer view about what really differs between valuation methods, it is necessary to start more generally by looking at what can be called 'the information base of a valuation'. A valuation method/approach can from this perspective be seen as consisting of two different parts:

1) A view about which type of information about the properties to use in the valuation.
2) A view about how this information should be processed in order to arrive at a market value.

In Tables 3.1 and 3.2, a list is presented of what can be the most relevant types of information (see Bellman 2018). As will be explained below, Table 3.1 focuses on somewhat more objective factors, while Table 3.2 focuses on other types of information.

Table 3.1 Potentially useful information (1): relatively more objective.

Category	Examples
1. Observed prices for properties sold	
2. Physical characteristics of the property and of comparable object	Area, status of technical systems (when they were renovated), environmental labels
3. Legal characteristics of the property and of comparable objects	Building rights according to land-use plan
4. Economic dimensions of the property and of comparable objects	Current and historical operating costs and revenues, cost for various improvements
5. The value of real estate companies on the stock market	Can be divided into companies with properties of different types

Table 3.2 Potentially useful information (2): relatively more subjective.

Category	Examples
6. Expectations about the future (for the property and comparable objects)	Future price
	How the physical characteristics will change of time
	How the legal rules will change
	Future revenue, future cost
	Future value of company on the stock market
	Possibility to change the property in the future (real options)
7. Inside information from earlier transactions	Reservation prices for sellers and different buyers, bids during the transaction process
8. Goals and strategies among actors on the market	How different actors evaluate, for example, risk and rates of return demand for different types of properties. Rules of thumbs used to determine a reasonable price. Gut feelings concerning different characteristics, e.g. that properties constructed in a certain way are riskier

The information in Table 3.1 is grouped into five categories. The first and most obvious type of information is observations about *recent prices for properties*. To be able to use the price information data about *physical characteristics*, e.g. areas of buildings, is important. Environmental classifications belong to this category as they typically are partly based on physical features of the property (materials, energy use etc.). The *legal rules* about the possible use of the building (and of comparable objects) are also important, and of course also a number of *economic dimensions* (e.g. current costs and revenues). In some countries, there are a number of real estate companies listed on the stock exchange and information about the value of these companies can potentially be of interest to value a specific property.

There are potential problems with all kinds of information, even these relatively more objective ones. The *stated price* might not be the actual price paid (especially in countries where there are transaction taxes related to the price paid). Various side-agreements between buyer and seller (e.g. loans from the seller) can be used to manipulate the price. *Areas* might be defined and measured in different ways. Direct fraud can also occur. Information about *costs* and *revenues* can also be manipulated, e.g. through different ways to allocate these costs over time. What should be classified as a cost, or expense, and what as an investment? *Stock market* manipulations are not unheard of. But the types of information in Table 3.1 could still be seen as relatively objective information.

In Table 3.2, more subjective information that can be relevant in determining market values is listed. This information is divided into three subcategories.

The first category concerns *expectations* about the future development of different variables. What a person is willing to pay for a property today should depend upon their expectations concerning all the variables above, e.g. future revenue and cost, the degradation process of the building, possible options in the form of changing the use of the land and the building, and of course the development of the real estate and stock market in general. These expectations are not observable in the same way as the information in Table 3.1, but a person working in the market that meets with a lot of persons in the sector can have a rather clear view of the expectations in the market. These views can be based on information given in discussions with both owners of properties and potential buyers in the market, but also on contacts with actors in the financial sector and government organizations.

A person that has been involved in earlier transactions, as buyer, seller, bidder or advisor, can have *inside information* about how actors on the market have behaved in earlier transactions, e.g. number of bidders, bids, bargaining strategies and approximate reservation prices for both buyers and sellers.

Contacts with actors on the market can also give more general information about the *goals and strategies of parties that are active on the market*. The information can be about how they evaluate risk for different kinds of properties, what rate of return they apply in the calculations about investment value, which in turn is relevant for determination of their reservation prices.

The kind of information described in Table 3.2 is typically less verifiable than the information presented in Table 3.1. If a valuation for some reason is questioned in court, it might be more difficult to present information of the type listed in Table 3.2 in a credible way. If less verifiable information is used in a valuation,

Table 3.3 IFRS Fair value hierarchy: quality of inputs.

Level	Inputs
1	Quoted prices (unadjusted) in active markets for identical assets or liabilities that the entity can access at the measurement date.
2	Inputs other than quoted prices ... that are observable for the asset or liability, either directly or indirectly and in need of minor adjustments.
3	Unobservable inputs for the asset or liability.

it also raises issues about the objectivity and transparency in a valuation, as will be discussed further in Chapter 8.

The types of information presented in the tables above can be related to what the IFRS call *the Fair Value hierarchy* that reflect their view of the quality of inputs to a valuation. Table 3.3 describes how these different inputs are classified.

The concept of 'unobservable' is problematic in this context as advisers that have participated in negotiations may have 'observed' a number of things that for other persons might seem to be unobservable, e.g. the rate of return demanded by important actors.

In this context, it is important to be aware of the distinction in contract theory between observable and verifiable. Something is verifiable only if it can convince a third party, e.g. a court. A party involved in a transaction may have observed something but there might be no evidence that would convince a court that this is true.[2] One interpretation of the Levels in Table 3.3 is then that data in Level 2 are observable and verifiable, while Level 3 data are observable but not (easily) verifiable. In the context of financial reporting, one probably also need to bear in mind that International Accounting Standards Board (IASB) primarily has the needs of a user (of financial reports) in mind when putting a label on inputs in valuation models.

Also important to bear in mind: when assets are valued applying Level 3-inputs in valuation models, there is also a risk that calculated values may reflect more of investment values or values in use from the point of view of a specific actor (see, e.g. Hitz 2007; Lind and Nordlund 2019). The estimated value may therefore not fully align with the definitions of market value and/or fair value. Criticism regarding fair (market) values estimated by applying Level 3-inputs in valuation models can also be found in Benston (2008) and Penman (2007).

---

2 Even though the distinction between observable and verifiable is a standard distinction in contract theory, it can be questioned, see Lind and Nyström (2011).

The information base of valuation is investigated in Bellman (2018) and her conclusion based on interviews with Swedish valuers is:

> Analyses of the data show that four types of information have the greatest impact on estimated market value: the *local environment* and *location* are perceived as reliable, and property appraisers have confidence in those assessments; *rental income* seems problematic, because the property owner is the major source of information; and property appraisers are not confident in assessments based on *discount rates*. (p. 1)

Local markets may, however, differ in the quality of specific data, so this conclusion concerning Sweden should only be seen as an example. Our point is primarily that valuers should have a clear view about the reliability of different types of information and take that into account when they select a method.

3.5 A Different Way to Classify Valuation Methods

The market value is defined as the most probable price if a property is sold. In the article 'A transparent two-step categorization of valuation method' (Lind and Nordlund 2014), we start with discussing how different variables can be linked to what happen on the market. Three options then seem possible.

3.5.1 The Sales Comparison Approach

The simplest way is of course to *make the link through recently observed prices*. A broad interpretation of a sales comparison or market approach is to define it as any method that uses information about recently observed prices. The observed prices can be normalized in a large number of ways – a large number of units of comparison can be used, typically some of the observable variables described in Table 3.1. This means, as argued above, that the gross and net capitalization method should be classified as a sales comparison method when capitalization rates are derived from observed transaction. If there is a relation between some measure of cost and observed prices, the cost can be used in a sales comparison approach.

3.5.2 Using Direct Information from the Actors

First, there is almost always a time-lag problem between transactions in the market and the value date. In the meantime, important things may have happened in the market that could affect market prices. For instance, financing deals could have been more difficult, or an unexpected essential event of some other kind could have happened that may lead to higher vacancies, lower rent appreciation-expectations etc. This means that other information than data from transactions are needed in most cases.

Especially in thin markets where there are few transactions, judgements about probable price can be based on more direct knowledge about how actors and potential actors 'think' and are reasoning. Firms that work with valuation and advice to investors can, for example, know what kind of calculations different actors make and how they view different risks. From that kind of information, the valuer can draw conclusions about the investor's probable willingness to pay for a specific property and this way may have a well-founded opinion about different actors bid-ask-spreads in the market. Lind and Nordlund (2014) discuss this under the heading 'actor-based methods'. Thorne[3] (2009, p. 14) makes the following comment on a similar issue 'The job of the valuer is to understand the market in which they operate. When transactions are thin on the ground, this means understanding the collective mindsets of would-be buyers and sellers, and of the fundamental economic drivers of that market. It means understanding why property that is being offered is not selling and at what price level buyers would enter the market'.

However, in this context, it is always important to bear in mind that actors in the market also must be able to transact at the price that is judged to be the market value (and fair value in accounting). In this respect, the knowledge about conditions for financing possible deals can have a very important impact. This includes knowledge about external providers of capital - their willingness to provide capital, e.g. a loan-to-value ratio – but also about the possibility to raise equity and the cost of different kinds of capital. The valuer could, for instance, ask: does the free cash flow yield suffice to service the debt (e.g. interest rate) and provide the holders of the equity instruments the return they require, e.g. dividend on shares? And will the value-appreciation of the property in the future give the required return to the owners not provided in pure cash flows by dividends?

The more heterogenous the actors are, and the larger the role of bargaining skills is, the more difficult it is to use an actor-based method. The actors may also have incentives to supply the valuer with biased information, if they think that this will be to their advantage in coming negotiations. We will return to these issues in Chapter 7 on transparency.

Banks and other providers of capital are also actors in the market with a business-interest in their decisions whether to provide capital or not. For instance, if the access to credit becomes easier and cheaper (lower interest rates and/or higher rates of debt-financing in deals), this would probably make it easier to pay more

---

3 Chris Thorne was Chairman of International Valuation Standards Board (IVSB) at that point in time.

for a property, and the other way around. Knowledge about the sentiment and behaviour of external capital providers is another example of essential knowledge to catch in an actor-based approach.

It may also be worth noting that valuers may need to consider what the most likely buyer category is for different types of real estate. Note, we do not aim at the most probable specific buyer here, we aim at the most probable category of buyer. The most probable specific buyer could be more driven by investment value than market value. Next, the appraiser needs to have an understanding of how price formation goes on for the particular type of item among actors in the category of probable buyers. For example, if the most likely buyer category is found among institutional investors, their purchase decision/investment decision may not be as dependent on the availability of credit capital as it may be when other buyer categories are most likely. Some investors are more driven by the return on equity while others are more driven by return on assets. Another example could be a smaller apartment building with, for example, four apartments where the most likely buyer category consists of actors who will use one of the apartments for their own accommodation and sees the rent from the three apartments rented by tenants as a contribution to his own housing cost. In short, the valuer needs to have knowledge of how different kinds of actor-categories form their price bids.

3.5.3 Using Data from the Stock Market

In the simplest case, there are companies listed on the stock market that only have a certain type of property. Changes in the value of these companies' equity-instruments should give some indication about the development of the value of properties that the company owns. Several studies – see, for example, Sebastian and Schätz (2009) and Hoesli and Oikarinen (2012) - show a sizeable positive correlation between the value of listed property shares and underlying real estate assets, at least in the longer term. In practice, however, valuers seem reluctant to use stock market data. Price discovery between private and public real estate markets are also discussed in Geltner et al. (2003).

In this context, it is interesting to note that IFRS 13 under the heading 'Level 2 inputs' addresses that inputs in this hierarchy level can be information derived in different ways from observable market data (market corroborated data). For instance, a relationship can be demonstrated by a correlation. In 2008 and 2009, it was discussed whether, in real estate valuation, one may (or even should) had drawn conclusions on the underlying real estate values from the fact that the share prices of listed property companies had fallen considerably in the preceding two years. As studies show a sizeable positive correlation between the value of listed property shares and underlying real estate assets in the longer term, a valuer should not ignore such observable input. It should be kept in mind that prices of equity-instruments listed on the stock exchange also could be driven by other things than the underlying value of the real estate assets. For instance, high or low confidence in the management of a company could affect share prices.

Different types of studies also imply that the stock market generally shows higher volatility than the underlying real asset market and that prices in the stock market also tend to react to information earlier than underlying real assets. Since volatility and timing issues show different patterns when comparing direct and indirect real estate assets, it is important in this context that the valuer also needs to take into account the time lag between pricing-listed real estate shares on the stock exchange and pricing regarding the underlying assets in the direct real estate market. This lack of direct connection between stock markets and real estate prices implies that it is difficult to get more than a rough indication of how the market value has changed from stock market data. In cases where there are few transactions on the real estate market, data from the stock market should be helpful at least to estimate the direction of change in the market.

An extreme case where we believe that stock-market data should have been used was in the beginning of the financial crisis in Sweden during the fall of 2008 when the transaction market for commercial properties dried up almost completely. Swedish valuers then, on many occasions, argued that since there were hardly any new transactions, there were no indications of a change in the market values. At the same time, the value of real estate companies (equity) fell on the stock market and consequently the implied values on underlying properties became lower. In such a case, it would have been rational to use stock-market data and at least make some reductions in the estimated market values, e.g. in financial reports.

3.6 Adjustment Methods

A very common situation is that the object to be valued has some special characteristics compared to objects upon which the sales comparison analysis is based - or compared to the objects that implicitly are used in an actor-based approach. This means that an adjustment must be made to reach the most probable price of the property in question. These adjustments can be based on several different methods (see, e.g. Lind and Nordlund 2014).

In some cases, it might be possible to interpolate between the observed prices using some kind of grid method (see, e.g. *The Appraisal of Real Estate* 2013, p. 401f). If, for example, price/sqm is used and one object is somewhat bigger and another somewhat smaller and that price/sqm varies between the two, then an interpolation could be used to find the best estimate of the price/sqm of the valuation object. An interpolation can, however, be made in different ways but if the interval is rather small, the difference between a linear and a non-linear interpolation should be small.

In other cases, the valuation object has characteristics that none of the transacted objects have. Then, one or more of the following methods can be used.

3.6.1 General Statistical Analysis

In the scientific literature, there are many statistical studies (hedonic studies) that investigate the effect of different variables on house prices all over the world. Even though they are made on other markets, they can give at least rough indications of the effect of the variable in question. For example, how a swimming pool affects the value of single-family houses or how a green label affects the value of a commercial property (see Chapter 7 on sustainability and property values). Combining this with local knowledge can give evidence for the size of the adjustment needed.

3.6.2 Using Discounted Cash-Flow Analysis for Valuing the Difference

If an income-producing property is valued, then there might be difference of type where a certain investment is needed in, say, three years in the comparison objects while it is not needed until after five years in the valuation object. In cases like this, an adjustment could be calculated by using a cash-flow analysis. If the (real) rate of return demanded is estimated to be 4% and the investment is 100, then the difference in the present value would be 7 (89–82). This way of making adjustment could be motivated by arguing that the actors on the market make this kind of calculation before buying or selling a property. This method is recommended by Rushmore (1992) for appraisal of hotel properties.

3.6.3 Costs and Rules of Thumb

An example: The building that is to be valuated has had the roof replaced recently while the buildings in the comparison objects still have old roofs. The cost of replacing the roof was 100. An old rule-of-thumb in Sweden is that if an improvement is made on a building, the market value increases with 50% of the cost. This rule is based on a very detailed study from the 1950s of farmhouses! There are also theoretical arguments suggesting that a rational buyer may not be willing to pay the full cost for various measures that the former owner has recently made. The buyer may be uncertain about the quality of the work – compared to if they had done it themselves. The buyer may also have preferred to do the work in a somewhat different way, e.g. build a somewhat different swimming pool or renovated the kitchen differently.

3.6.4 Actor-Based Approach

The methods described above for making adjustment all include an element of judgement from people that are knowledgeable about the situation in the specific market. However, adjustments can also be made based on a more extreme version of an 'actor-based' approach. An experienced valuer or broker may have a clear feeling about how the value of an object would change if a certain characteristic changes, even if this intuition cannot be related to any specific empirical evidence. From the perspective of objectivity and transparency, this, however, creates problem that we will return to in Chapter 8.

3.7 Why Is Regression Analysis (Hedonic Methods) Seldom Used in Ordinary Valuations?

The price that is paid for a property is determined by a number of characteristics of the property, each of them affecting the value of the property. A natural idea is then that the property value can be determined by the use of statistical methods. By regressing observed prices against information about the characteristics of the transacted properties, it should be possible to find the effect of the variables. If we have estimated an equation that describes how the price is related to the value-determining characteristics, such an equation could be used to determine the expected price for any property in the market that the study covers.

During at least the last 50 years, a large number of statistical studies of price determinants have been made. Time and again there are beliefs that statistical methods/regression analysis/hedonic studies will replace traditional valuation methods, and it is interesting to think about why this has not happened on a larger scale.

For mass valuation purposes, e.g. taxation, the statistical methods have been used in many countries for many years. They have also been used in Automated Valuation Models (AVM), for example when banks make rough valuations of standard residential houses and apartments for lending purposes. The development in the area of Artificial Intelligence can be expected to improve these 'automatic valuation methods' further: see Chapter 10 on the future of valuation.[4]

---

4 A recent overview of methods used can be found in d'Amato and Kauko (2017) or in Grover (2016).

The dominating valuation methods are, however, still characterized by the use of a smaller number of comparable properties, and then making various adjustments (see Section 3.6) instead of making a statistical analysis of a larger number of transactions. An illuminating discussion about this can be found in the article 'Error trade-offs in regression analysis appraisal methods' by Kummerow and Galfalvy (2002).

The arguments in that article can be summarized in the following way. Using only the most similar objects, typically 3–5 objects, there is a higher risk of random errors. It might have been the case that in these specific transactions, the number of interested parties was either higher or lower than usual. By adding more observations, the risk of these random errors is reduced. On the other hand, adding more objects that might differ in new ways (e.g. more distant from the valuation object), then the effects of more variables need to be estimated. Suppose we start with a small number of observations from District A, and that we think about adding observations from District B, then it is necessary to include a variable in the equation to take into account the effect of the difference between Districts A and B. The more objects we add, the less likely is it that there are stable relations between the variables and the price. The effect of a certain characteristic, e.g. size of a building, may differ between the districts, and then new (dummy) variables might be needed and then the precision of the estimate may not increase even though more objects are included.

There are also many uncertainties when using statistical methods, e.g. concerning what to include in the equation and how different factors interact. If these uncertainties are believed to be larger than the uncertainty related to random factors, then it is rational to only use a smaller number of the most similar properties and then try to make various adjustments using methods like the ones described above.

This discussion can be compared to a discussion about evaluation methods in general (see, e.g. Bohm and Lind 1993). Suppose you want to find out the effect of a tax change on employment (as in that study). One strategy is to formulate a general equation about employment-determining factors and add tax level as one such factor, and then use regression analysis to identify the effect of the tax. The other strategy is to use what is called a quasi-experimental approach, where the researcher tries to find companies and regions that are as similar as possible to the companies/regions where the tax is reduced but where there has been no tax reduction. This quasi-experimental approach for evaluation of effects is structurally very similar to the valuation methods where only a small number of 'very' similar objects are used to estimate the market value. The advantage is in both cases that it is not necessary to evaluate the effect of the (large number of) factors that the objects have in common.

In their article, Kummerow and Galfalvy describe their conclusions in the following way:

> This paper implies that we will never be able to estimate property prices very precisely by hedonic methods, or any other method due to the nature of reality. Errors will often be large and ill-behaved because pricing processes are messy, diverse, and complex. Furthermore, it is impossible to quantify significant misspecification and measurement errors. The problem is not in the statistics but in the states of nature.

But in theory, the situation could also be the other way around, with large random factors in the observed sales but stable underlying relations between a small number of factors. In such a case, some kind of hedonic method can give a more credible result.

3.8 What Is Really the Cash-Flow Method?

3.8.1 How Can the Cash-Flow Method Give a Market Value?

The cash-flow method is often mentioned as one of the methods within the income approach to property valuation. The basic idea in the cash-flow method is to estimate the value of the property by discounting future cash-flows (revenue and expenses, and a future exit value). This method is the obvious one to use if the aim is to estimate an investment value from the perspective of a specific actor. It is a way for a potential buyer to estimate their maximum willingness to pay, or for an owner to estimate the minimum price that they would be willing to sell the property for.

McParland et al. (2002) and Bellman and Lind (2018) show that especially in the Nordic countries, property valuers say that the cash-flow method is the valuation method that they most often use for estimating a market value. The question in this section is how this can be possible? How can the valuer argue that the result of the cash-flow analysis really is the market value? It is well known that rather small changes in the assumptions in a cash-flow analysis can lead to rather large differences in results, and how can the valuer know which assumptions lead to the market value?[5] There are several possible arguments here.

One argument is that the valuer could get the market value instead of the investment value by *replacing the individual investor's beliefs about the future with the general beliefs of the actors on the market*. This idea could be found in the

---

5 This critique can e.g. be found in *The Appraisal of Real Estate* (2013) p. 530.

quotation from IVSC (2019) presented earlier in the chapter and also in French (2012). The cash-flow method would then be an example of an actor-based method. A major problem is, however, whether there are any 'market beliefs' about future rents and operating costs, reasonable rates of return and value of the property in X years (the exit value). Potential investors can be expected to have very different views of the future and what is then the beliefs of the 'market'? And even if they have similar views on the value of the object, they may have different views about the specific components. One actor might believe that rents will rise, but that the risk is rather large, while another does not think that rents will increase, but also that the risk is rather small. The differences in beliefs cancel out and they have the same belief about what is the reasonable price.

It is sometimes argued that the numbers in the cash-flow calculation are derived from observed transactions on the market, but this is not possible. If it is observed that a transaction occurs at a specific price, it is not possible to derive a unique set of underlying values as *many combinations of inputs can lead to the same price.*

Nordlund (2008) and Bellman and Lind (2018) point to another possible interpretation of the discounted cash-flow method as a method for market valuation. They argue that the cash-flow method as used in Sweden can be seen as a somewhat more sophisticated version of the direct capitalization methods. Suppose that the valuer in the cash-flow analysis assumes, as they typically do in Sweden, that rents and operating costs follow inflation, and that the exit value is calculated from the NOI at the end of the period. The outcome of such a calculation will normally be that NOI appreciates with the assumed inflation rate and that the residual value (exit value) as well appreciated with the assumed inflation rate. Hence, in real terms, the cash flows will be of the same amount each year and the residual (exit value) will be at the same level as when the calculation starts (in real terms). *Given these assumptions, there is really only one 'unknown' in the equation – the discount rate - and the discount rate can then be derived from the observable information* about price and NOI in year 1 and the assumed inflation. This is illustrated in the formula below with the discount rate as x as the only unknown.

$$\text{Observed price} = \sum_{i=1}^{n} \frac{NOI(1+in)^{i}}{(1+x)^{i}} + \frac{NOI(1+in)^{n}}{(1+x-in)^{n}}.$$

NOI = net operating income
x = rate of return
in = inflation rate

Before the derivation of the rate of return is carried out, the NOI is 'normalized' in order to make it more likely to find a stable rate of return.

Technically, it is therefore possible to derive this 'market discount rate' from observed transactions and this discount rate can then be used to estimate a market value for the property that is to be valued. This issue is also discussed in Morri and Benedetto (2019, p. 81f).

When the rate of return has been derived, the formula can also be used to make further adjustments to the estimated value. For example, if the contracted rent is lower/higher than the normalized rent, then the estimated value will be adjusted. Adjustments could also be made if there is need for major renovations in the way described above when DCF-methods are used for adjustments.

The general conclusion from this is that when the DCF-method is used for estimating the market value, it can be seen as a version of the net capitalization method, with the advantage that the explicit structure makes it easy to make adjustments for special features of the property to be valued. As French and Sloane (2018, p. 405) puts it, 'Rather than seeing implicit and explicit models as "rivals", they should be seen as two sides of the same coin'.

3.8.2 Problems When Using Accounting Data in Valuations

When discussing the cash-flow method in a valuation context, it is important to note how cash flows are defined and measured, especially when data from different companies are used.

A valuer needs to take into account that NOI derived from accounting information may be incorrect in that it is not a true cash-flow figure. Payments can be capitalized if they are seen as reinvestment to maintain the return capacity of the property. Often, this is not easy to obtain information about. The easily accessible NOI from an income statement may lack the cash outflows necessary to keep the property updated and attractive in the market, if only repairs (day-to-day servicing and replacement of minor parts) are expensed in the income statement. The reported NOI might then overestimate the true NOI as some expenses are not included. This might lead to an overestimation of the yield and, consequently, that the risk reimbursement in reality is lower than it seems to be. The gap between yields on property and the risk-free interest rate is overstated.

There are then problems to get an idea of the cash-flow capacity for properties from accounting information. Two common ways of gathering such information are:

1) Net operating income = Rent less operation and maintenance (often derived from income statement information, i.e. revenue less operating - and maintenance expensed in the income statement depending on which accounting rules are followed).

2) Free operating cash flow = Rent reduced by cost of operation and maintenance but also reduced by reinvestments (capital expenditure) which are necessary to maintain the return on investment. As mentioned, these reinvestments are often capitalized and accounted for in the balance sheet and not in the income statement. Regardless of how these costs are accounted for, they are cash outflows that need to be taken into consideration when evaluating the free cash-flow capacity of an investment (e.g. a property). To make it possible to find this information, the property companies should give good information in notes to the accounts about the nature of different capital expenditure outflows. This includes acquired properties that increase the rentable area of the whole company, newly erected buildings or extension of buildings that have the same effect as acquisitions and finally reinvestments in owned properties needed to keep these assets attractive in the market.

The normal formula for the adequate cash flow to use in valuation models is:

$$\begin{aligned} \text{Free operating cash flow} = {} & \text{Operating profit} \left(\text{sometimes named EBIT}\right) + \text{depreciation} \\ & \left(\text{where applicable}\right) - \text{reinvestments needed to maintain return capacity} \left(\text{capex}\right) \\ & \pm \text{changes in working capital} \end{aligned}$$

These accounting-related problems and the concept 'free cash flow yields' are discussed more in detail in Young et al. (2017), Reid (2019) and Nordlund (2014). In Chapter 6, there are further discussions regarding accounting information, reported NOI in income statements and cash-flow estimations. In general, it is very important when using information from income statements to investigate what kind of yield or cash flow that are presented as companies may handle these issues in different ways. The valuer must make sure that data about different properties really are comparable.

3.9 Valuation of Development Properties and Option Aspects

3.9.1 Development Properties – Some General Issues

Valuation of development properties and properties with enhancement possibilities are examples of problematic valuation situations with lack of data and high uncertainty (see, e.g. Crosby et al. 2018). This concerns valuation of properties during the construction period and valuation of building rights connected to a piece of land. It could also be noted here that the IFRS-standard IAS 40 on

Investment property normally requires that investment properties under construction, or properties developed for future use as investment properties, should be valued at fair value (market value). This value should be estimated continually in financial reports. See IAS 40 para 8 e (and Chapter 6).

Two methods have, on many occasions, been described as suitable for solving such valuation issues:

Method 1. A direct sales comparison approach. The market value of the land (including building right or potential such rights) with any existing building at the time of value plus costs incurred for new construction or conversion is valued from prices in recent transactions of similar properties. The problem with this approach is that there normally are very few such transactions and even if there are some transactions, the objects are typically very heterogenous. When we reach the stage that the building process has been started up, it is even more difficult to find observable transaction information about similar projects in the same phase of construction as the specific development project. However, one should also bear in mind that estimating a market value is about estimating an exit price in the market. If there is a combination of observed land prices and costs incurred up to the valuation date, it could be argued that this is a mixture between entry price (costs incurred) and exit price (market value of land/building rights and any existing building).

Method 2. A combination of a sales comparison approach and a cost approach, as mentioned in Section 3.2. In this case, the market value of development property is determined as the difference between the market value of the property in finished condition minus the remaining costs for completing the building. This method is also problematic from the perspective of the definition of market value, as there is a combination of a market value (for the finalized project) and an entry price in the form of costs that is expected to be occurred.

If there is an estimated project gain, it could be argued that such a gain in a bargaining situation probably would be split between sellers and buyers in a market where actors are rational. Method 2 is built on the assumption that if the property is sold during the construction period, the entire profit from the project ends up with the seller. If a rational actor was to buy an ongoing project and enter into the risk it entails, it would be rational to think that the buyer would like to have a share of the project profit above the normal profit.

It is also clear that whatever methods are used, the valuation of development properties is very uncertain, not the least because it is a thin market and where actors can be expected to have rather different opinions about both the future market value of the finalized property and the remaining cost. Small changes in these figures can lead to large changes in the value of development property. An example: If the value of the finalized building is estimated to be 100 and remaining construction costs 80, then the value of the development property would be 20. If both inputs are changed with 10% in opposite direction, this value of the development property would fall with 90% to 2 (90–88).

3.9.2 Real Options Aspects

As noted in the discussion about highest and best use in the last chapter, a property typically includes a number of (real) options and one important issue is how options affect the value and how valuers can take this into account.

A real option can in this context be seen as a (more or less certain) possibility to change the property in one way or another (see, e.g. Pomykacz and Olmsted 2013). The simplest example is that the use of a property can be changed. An office building may be changed to housing, or the other way around. A shopping centre - or a part of a shopping centre – may be demolished and replaced by housing, when the demand for retail space falls as a consequence of growing trade volumes through the Internet. In a world of uncertainty, an investor should be willing to pay extra for a property that includes such options compared to a property that does not.

Let us take the shopping-centre case as an example. Suppose that the investors compare two different centres (A and B). In both cases, we can imagine that demand has fallen and that there are some vacant spaces. The value as a shopping centre is assumed to be the same in both cases. Shopping centre A is, however, located in an area where house prices are low or have fallen, while house prices around centre B are high and/or rising. Centre A also has a physical structure that makes it difficult to demolish it. The possibility to get a planning permit to change the use from retail to housing may also differ. Even if it is not profitable today to change the use of any of the centres, a rational investor would be willing to pay considerably more for a centre, where there is a high probability that planning permits would be given, where conversion cost is low and where the value of housing properties is high. One important thing when considering options of different kinds is to evaluate whether the option could be 'in the money' – that is, for example, when the cost of demolishing the old building together with the cost of construction for a new building is lower than the value of the new building when completed.

Valuation might also be affected when contracts include options. Both French (2001) and Vimpari (2018) discuss how rental contracts including options to renew or option to downscale can be valued.

The development of the Black-Sholes formula for valuing options led to a Nobel Prize in Economics in 1997. This formula, however, uses data that typically are not available for the kind of options discussed and simpler methods have been recommended, see for example French (2001). The general idea is instead to make a decision tree and evaluate how valuable the property would be if different situations occur and then set probabilities on the different possible outcomes.

There might not be any special problems when valuing a property with certain real options. Using a comparative sales approach and objects that are very similar to the property to be valued and located rather close to that property, it may be expected that the properties have the same real options. Then the observed transaction prices would already include how 'the market' values the options that the buildings include. As discussed in the last chapter, there might be very different views on what can be done with a building and this can create more random price differences for properties with options, depending on the views of specific potential buyers.

On a more heterogenous market, it is more important for the valuer to investigate if the properties differ in the options available and the value of these options. Different methods of adjustment are described above. However, it is probable that knowledge about how the actors think is more important to evaluate how much higher/lower the value might be as a result of differences in the options available.

3.10   Use of Different Methods in the Valuation of a Specific Object: Concluding Comments

All property valuation models lead to uncertain results as discussed more in the next chapter. One idea that can be found in the literature is that this uncertainty can be reduced by using different methods and then weighting the results from the different methods to get a final result.[6] In a study about valuations before and after the dramatic financial crisis in Sweden in the early 1990s, this question was investigated (Ekelid et al. 1998). They found that after the crises valuers to a larger extent reported the result from both a sales comparison approach and from some kind of income method. The impression from the valuation reports was that using two different methods was seen as giving more reliable valuations.

A problem was, however, observed. In turned out that the result from the different methods often led to very similar results, with a difference between them often below 5%. But if all valuation methods are uncertain and you actually use two different and independent methods, it should often be a case that the gap between the results of the different methods is rather large. No case was found where the valuer reported large differences in results depending on which method was used. Interviews with valuers also showed that the methods really were not independent and that various adjustments had been made in order to make the results more

---

6 D'Amato (2018) discusses how such a reconciliation between methods can be formalized.

similar. This meant that it was not really two independent methods. That the results were similar was not a strong argument for a higher reliability in the presented market value. Especially, as no information was given about the adjustments made during the valuation process. The transparency of the valuation was therefore low.

The most general recommendation from this chapter is that it is *better to think in terms of information bases and strategies of information processing than to think in terms of a small number of specific valuation methods.*

The information that a valuer can employ concerns relatively more observable data like prices paid, rent and operating costs. But the experienced valuer also uses more general but less verifiable knowledge about how investors in the market think and what feature of a property they typically like and dislike. It should be underlined that there is uncertainty in all kinds of data, relating to everything from simple mistakes in the book-keeping to fraud. There is also a need to constantly update the more informal information about actors on the market as investors and banks may change their minds quickly. Some old investors might disappear from the market and new ones show up, and this makes experience from earlier transactions less relevant.

What is usually called different methods could perhaps better be described as different strategies to be used for specific situations where certain information is lacking. As especially commercial properties are so heterogenous and the number of transactions relatively small, there is a need to use all types of information, but in a systematic way. The fair-value hierarchy (discussed above in the context of IFRS 13) illustrates this and the typical formulation in the American literature that the different approaches should be used together points in the same direction.

This way of thinking also has the advantage that it opens up for more creativity. Given certain available information and a certain type of property, there might be new strategies for estimating a credible probable price. One should not think in terms of a given number of predetermined and well-defined 'methods' to find a market value. It is, however, not far from the truth to say that everything is really about analysing information from the transaction market, but not only data from actual transactions. Thorne (2009) comments that 'a figure arrived at using a robust rationale based on thorough market understanding is generally more reliable than one based on a stale comparable transaction' (p. 14). In our view, evidence from prices in transactions is desirable but such evidence is far from an absolute requirement, especially in smaller markets where actors for strategic reason may not carry out any transactions when demand has fallen. Actor-based methods discussed above and methods using data from the stock market can from this perspective be seen as giving information that can be used to interpret and make adjustments to the data from the most recent transactions.

Based on the discussion above, transparency in the property transaction market is essential for good valuations. However, the real estate transaction market is surrounded by a variety of problems and obstacles. In many countries, an essential part of the transactions in later years were so-called wrappers or other kinds of indirect sales. Equity instruments in companies holding a property, or properties, are traded instead of the property itself. This means that information about prices in transactions gets opaque due to the way transactions are made in the property market. Instead, there are prices on equity-instruments of companies holding properties, and from such information, if available, underlying property values should be estimated. There is, however, no easy way to do this. Sales-contracts for equity instruments are seldom or never public information. Furthermore, all transactions are not automatically representative for estimating market values with a comparable sales method without further/deeper analysis of the circumstances in the specific situation. In this respect, see, for instance, discussions in Bretten and Wyatt (2001), Lind and Nordlund (2019), and Goetzmann and Peng (2006).

Exercises

1 Investigate what valuation methods are used by local valuers? How do they look at the reliability of different methods? To what extent do they depend on 'inside information' from earlier transactions that they participated in? How do they use the discounted cash-flow model? What kind of data are available and used? Do they use a different method and how is the final result arrived at in such a case?

2 If commercial properties often are sold as companies, how do the valuer handle this? What kind of adjustments are made? How are tax aspects handled?

3 You are going to make an estimation of market value for an investment property at the value date. In the illustration below you can see an index for a time sequence showing comparable sales development (*) and implied values on properties (the line) extracted from traded equity instruments on the stock exchange for companies holding similar properties as the valuation object and the comparable sales. You can also see Bid-Ask spreads at different points in time according to your knowledge about actors in the market who are potential buyers and sellers for such properties as the valuation object. You can also see banks' willingness to finance deals with such properties at different points in time as a Loan-To-Value (LTV) ratio. Discuss how to make a market value

estimate at the value-date based on knowledge of this information from the market. What market value figure would you suggest (expressed as an index-level, e.g. 120, 100, 80)?

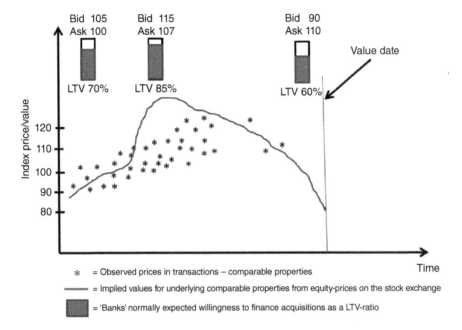

* = Observed prices in transactions – comparable properties

—— = Implied values for underlying comparable properties from equity-prices on the stock exchange

▮ = 'Banks' normally expected willingness to finance acquisitions as a LTV-ratio

4

Uncertainty and Bias in Property Valuations

4.1 Introduction

After a crash on a real estate market, there are often heated discussions about the quality of property valuations. One central issue is then uncertainty in valuations and how uncertainty is described in valuation reports. Investors who have lost money on their investments try to blame the valuers and argue that the valuers should have warned them that prices might fall. The valuers should have indicated that it might be irrational to pay the high prices that the investor actually paid! The Mallinson report in the United Kingdom in the 1990s was made after such a crash and treatment of uncertainty in valuation was a central issue in that report (Mallinson 1994). There has also been a large academic debate about uncertainty in property valuations during the last 30 years.

Looking at the standard textbooks, the following distinctions and comments can be found. Wyatt (2013) makes a distinction between the following two aspects of uncertainty (p. 349):

- *Valuation variance*: that different valuers come to different conclusions about the value of a specific property even if they have the same information.
- *Valuation inaccuracy*: that the estimated market value differs from the sales price.

Baum and Crosby (2008) discuss *valuation accuracy* (p. 20) but also *bias and smoothing*. They write that there is 'a substantial research literature that reinforces the perception that valuations both lag the market and smooth the peaks and throughs of "real" prices' (p. 21). They also note that bias can be the result of client influence (p. 22).

In *'The Appraisal of Real Estate'* (2013, chapter 14), uncertainty is primarily discussed in the context of statistical methods and the estimation of confidence intervals.

Advanced Issues in Property Valuation, First Edition. Hans Lind and Bo Nordlund.
© 2021 John Wiley & Sons Ltd. Published 2021 by John Wiley & Sons Ltd.

IVSC (2019, p. 14) does not say more than that *significant* uncertainty, e.g. concerning future cash-flows, should be disclosed in the valuation report.

RICS has published guidance notes concerning uncertainty (RICS 2019, p. 116–117) and pointed out circumstances where uncertainty can be expected to be higher, e.g. if the object is unique or where there are real options involved (potential planning permits/enhancement possibilities). Lack of information and disruptions on the market can also increase uncertainty. We will return to their recommendations about how uncertainty should – or should not – be reported in the final section of this chapter.

When looking at the academic discussion about valuation uncertainty, one can find at least two more interpretations beside valuation variance and valuation accuracy:

1) *Strength of evidence*: even if all valuers agree about the market value, they might in some cases be very convinced that the result really is the most probable price, while they in other cases are much more uncertain, as the evidence is not so strong.
2) *Valuation stability*: especially in the German literature, valuation uncertainty also covers discussions about the risk that the price will fall after the date of valuation. Saying that a market value is uncertain then indicates that the probability of a change in the price is high, and especially that a fall in the price is more likely.

In Sections 4.2–4.5, these four different interpretations will be discussed and in the end of the chapter, some possible recommendations will be discussed.

That a property valuation is uncertain can be interpreted as that the valuation on average is correct, but that the market value might be somewhat higher or somewhat lower than the estimated one. The dispersion of observed prices around the estimated market value might be rather large, but the estimation of the most probable price is still correct. Another related issue mentioned by Baum and Crosby above concerns bias: *That there might be systematic differences between the estimated market value and the true market value.* This difference might be in either direction: overestimation or underestimation. Several mechanisms can cause such a bias, e.g.

- *Client influence*: The client may try to pressure the valuer in a certain direction.
- *Behavioural factors*: That valuers follow certain rules of thumb that can lead to biased results.
- *Valuation smoothing:* That the use of earlier transaction or valuations lead to a smoother development than the true one.

- *Self-selection*: As transactions are voluntary, the transacted properties may not be representative of the stock and therefore give a biased picture of the rate of return on properties.

These different potential causes of bias are discussed in Sections 4.6–4.9.

4.2 Valuation Variance: Why Do Valuers Disagree?

There have been a number of experiments where a group of valuers are given a certain amount of information and then are given the task of valuing this specific property. Such experiments can, for example, be found in Adair et al. (1996).[1] These experiments typically show relatively large differences in the estimated value.

There are several possible explanations for such differences:

1) Different competence and skill among the valuers. There is, so to speak, one correct answer, or a rather narrow correct interval, and all the competent valuers agree that the market value is in that narrow interval. Some valuers are not as competent, and they draw wrong conclusions from the material and come to materially different conclusions.

2) The evidence is rather diverse and do not point clearly in a certain direction. If there is a limited amount of information and some differences between the properties that have been sold and the object to be valued now, then the valuers have to interpolate and extrapolate in several dimensions. Interpolations and extrapolations can be done in several different ways, all of which are consistent with the observations. Should the relations between characteristics of the property and the value of the property, in a certain interval, be linear or non-linear, and if it is non-linear, in which way? Even if there may exist research about these relations, this research cannot be expected to be conclusive and there is still a need to evaluate the relevance of these results for the specific market studied. The result of limited evidence is that there might be different opinions/estimations of market value even between very competent valuers. The valuers are, so to speak, using different mental models when making the valuations and even if these mental models could be made explicit, it might still not be possible to present evidence that indicates that one mental model is clearly better than the other ones. A special case of such differences in mental models can be that a valuer may be more or less optimistic about the development on the specific property market.

---

1 A critical examination of empirical studies about valuation variance and behavioural factors can be found in Klamer et al. (2017).

3) A third possible explanation for differences in valuation results may be more or less overt client pressure or be the result of other kind of biases discussed in Sections 4.6–4.9.

Finally, one must remember that agreement is not necessarily a sign of high quality in situations where uncertainty is high. In an uncertain situation, agreements among experts can in extreme cases be seen as a conspiracy where experts give the same answers even though there can be almost as strong arguments for another answers. When economic forecasts are discussed, the term 'cock-tail party effect' has been used to describe how the forecasters initially make rather different forecasts, but when they have met each other at some cocktail-parties, their forecasts converge and in the end, the forecasts are rather similar. Risk-aversion among the experts can also make them treat information in the same way and make similar predictions as no one wants to be the only one to make a forecast that turns out to be very wrong. If all are wrong in the same way, they can blame special circumstances. Therefore, they converge towards a certain answer, even though the evidence for this specific answer is not very strong. This is an example of what is called *herd behaviour* in the behavioural literature that we will return to in Section 4.7.

4.3 Valuation Accuracy: Why Do the Observed Price Differ from the Market Value?

Differences between the market value and the price have, as mentioned above, been labelled 'valuation accuracy'. It can be argued that this is not a very good term as it indicates that we should expect that the market value and the observed price are very close to each other. There are, however, no strong arguments for expecting that, especially in situations where the evidence for a certain market value is rather weak. There are a number of reasons why the observed price can differ from the estimated market value (the most probable price), even if it is assumed that the market value was estimated in the best possible way by competent valuers, and assuming that the transaction price is reported correctly (for instance, no direct or indirect side-payments, no synergies only relevant for a certain buyer or other agreements affecting the price). Differences between valuations and prices have also been discussed from a legal perspective as courts have discussed in terms of a reasonable margin of error within which the valuer cannot be faulted (see Crosby et al. 2000; Crosby 2000).

The first reason for a difference between market value and observed price is *that the distribution of reservation prices might differ*. This is easiest to illustrate if the property is sold through a standard ascending English auction. Suppose that the market value has been estimated to be 100 but that the market is rather thin with considerable differences in reservation prices between potential buyers. Let us assume that towards the end of the auction four potential buyers remain. Table 4.1 describes the reservation prices in two assumed cases. Notice that in both cases the highest and the lowest reservation prices are the same, and that the interval is rather narrow.

In Case 1, bidding would stop just above 95 and in the second case, just above 105. This example illustrates that rather *small differences in the distribution of reservation prices can lead to relatively large differences in observed prices*, even though the most probable price can be the same in both cases.

A second reason why the observed price can differ from the market value is *that the skills and bargaining power of the buyer and seller differ*. A skilled buyer that negotiates with an unskilled seller might be able to find arguments about problems in the property, and argue that the property actually is worse than the average property of that type and that it therefore is not reasonable to pay the estimated market value for this specific property. In another case, a skilled seller can find arguments that the property is better than average and convince a less-skilled buyer to accept a price above the estimated market value. If it is assumed that towards the end of the sales process there is one possible buyer with the highest reservation price and an interval between the lowest acceptable price for the seller and the highest acceptable price of the buyer, a skilled seller can push the price towards the maximum willingness to pay of the buyer. In the example in Table 4.1, a skilled seller may be able to push up the price close to 110. A skilled buyer can on the other hand push it down towards the lowest acceptable price for the seller. In Table 4.1, this would mean a price of 95 in Case 1 and 105 in Case 2. In a thin market, the difference between the two reservation prices can be rather large and in such a case, bargaining power can influence the outcome significantly.

It can also be that perceived deficiencies in a property, for example, a facade in need of renovation, are priced differently when it is the buyer's market in a recession and when it is the seller's market in the boom. In a boom, some potential

Table 4.1 Example of effects on price of the distribution of reservation prices.

	Reservation price Case 1	Reservation price Case 2
Bidder 1	90	90
Bidder 2	94	90
Bidder 3	95	105
Bidder 4	110	110

buyers may be very optimistic and this can be difficult to capture in the estimation of the probable price: See also Section 4.7.

These arguments lead us to expect that even though the average of the observed prices might be equal to the market value, there could in individual cases be rather large differences.

In a world of limited evidence, and where actors on the market make different assessments both concerning a specific property and concerning the development of the local market, it would actually be rather strange if observed prices most of the time are close to the estimated market value. There might, however, be institutional practices that push market values and observed prices closer to each other. Suppose, for example, that a company that plans to sell a property has an internal directive saying that the manager is not allowed to sell below estimated market value. The company that plans to buy has a similar internal directive saying that they are not allowed to buy at a higher price than the market value. If many companies have rules like this, then in extreme cases, all observed prices will be equal to the estimated market value. This is like a self-fulfilling prophecy as the observed prices then feed into the next valuation and confirm the original valuation. If the underlying individual investment value falls, the first thing that would happen is that the transaction volumes would go down. After a while someone would have to sell below the 'old' market value. The adjustments in observed prices to changing circumstances would in such a market be rather slow and it will take time before the prices move towards a new market value that better reflects the underlying investment values. As discussed in Chapter 2, changes in market conditions can in some situations lead to larger changes in turnover than in observed prices.

4.4   How Confident Is the Valuer in the Estimated Market Value?

The concept of probability can, as discussed in Chapter 2, be interpreted in terms of *how sure the expert is about the estimated market value and/or how strong the evidence for a certain value is.* Saying that the probability is high for a certain market value, then means that the valuers are very sure that the price will end up close to the estimated market value.

We can construct two cases where a group of valuers in both cases agree about the market value, but where the confidence in the value differs. There is then no valuation variance as defined above. *The strength of evidence* differs between the two cases. A simple illustration can be found in Table 4.2. In both cases, it is assumed that there are four recent sales of similar properties and that the estimated market value in both cases is 100. In the first case, the variance among the

Table 4.2 Different degrees of confidence in the estimated market value.

	Observed prices Case 1 with high confidence	Observed prices Case 2 with low confidence
Sale 1	95	80
Sale 2	100	95
Sale 3	100	105
Sale 4	105	120

observed transaction prices is low and therefore the confidence in the estimated market value is strong. In the second case, there is a larger variance between observed prices. In the second case, random factors - like one transaction more or less - could affect the estimated market value. If, for example, the transaction with the highest price had not been carried out, the market value may have been estimated to 98 in Case 1, while it could fall to 95 in the second case.

Strength of evidence can be evaluated for all the methods discussed in the last chapter. In some markets, there may, for example, be a very stable relation between rents and prices. In other markets, there might be a large spread in this relation. The same can hold for the estimated yield. As argued above, in a thin market, random factors and bargaining power can affect the final price, and this will also affect observed gross or net capitalization factors, or the rate of return used for calculating the 'market-adjusted' discounted cash flow. In some cases, the investors on a specific market might be rather homogenous and roughly calculate their investment value in the same way. In other cases, there might be a more heterogenous investor group that estimates its investment values rather differently. If there are investors from different countries with different opportunities on their home market, then more heterogeneity should be expected.

There should be a relation between strength of evidence and valuation 'accuracy': the stronger the evidence is the more likely should it be that the transaction price will end up close to the estimated market value. As will be returned to in Section 4.10, a qualitative report on the strength of evidence is one way of presenting uncertainty in valuation reports.

4.5 How Stable Is the Estimated Market Value?

In the Anglo-Saxon literature, a valuation is typically seen as a perishable good. The valuer estimates the market value at a specific date and there are no explicit and implicit statements about what the value of the property will be on a future date. There might even be explicit disclaimers in valuation reports underlining that the presented figure is an estimation of the market value at time t and that the report does not say anything about the market value at time t+i. Ekelid et al. (1998) note that these disclaimers increased in Sweden during the later phases of the boom in the late 1980s.

From a theoretical perspective, the view that the valuer should only estimate the current market value is rational *if the efficient market theory is true.* In an efficient market, the current prices reflect all available information and the best available theories. An important implication of the efficient market theory is that prices cannot be predicted as price changes only occur when there is genuinely new information - and such information can by definition not be predicted. There are several different interpretations of efficiency in this context, depending on what kind of information that is assumed to be known, but these details do not matter for the argument here. The central conclusion from the perspective of property valuation is that if the future price is impossible to predict, then it is rather meaningless to discuss if it is probable that the market value will fall or if the market value will rise in the near future. It is simply impossible to know and the valuer should not say anything about the value after the day of valuation.

The efficient market theory is, however, a controversial theory. One of the foremost critics is the Nobel laureate Robert Shiller who has argued both that asset prices fluctuate more than what can be motivated by the underlying income streams and that there is mean reversion in the statistical time series (see, e.g. his Nobel lecture, Shiller 2014). Mean reversions indicate there is a cyclical pattern in the data, where the probability of a fall in prices are higher when prices have risen, and that the probability of an increase in prices is higher if the prices have fallen. If there is such a pattern in the historical data, and if it is believed that the historical patterns still are relevant, then at least something can be said about the probable future development of the market value. A problem that has been discussed in this context is that if the market is at least to some extent predictable, then actors are in some sense irrational. If the prediction is that the market will go down, then why are some people paying a price that should lead to losses?

In the academic literature about property valuation, the willingness to discuss *risk in terms of probability of a change in market values* in a certain direction is higher among researchers in a German tradition (see, e.g. Lorenz et al. 2006). The question of uncertainty is in that literature treated as part of a *risk analysis*. In Lorenz et al. (2006), these risks are divided into the following categories (with a number of subcategories): 'market risk', 'location risk', 'property risk' and 'quality of the property cash flow'. The idea is that an investor can rate a specific property in these different dimensions, and that such a risk analysis would, for example, give some indication about how probable it is that the market value of that specific property will fall in the future.

It is, however, not completely clear how these risks shall be interpreted. In the theoretical literature, higher risk means higher variance in outcomes: both very good and very bad outcomes are possible. But risk analysis in the type of article mentioned above seems to be more focused on risk in a more common-sense interpretation, where a high risk means a high probability that the outcome will be worse than expected.

In the end, the controversy between those who believe in the efficient market theory and those who believe that future market values are predictable, at least in terms of direction, is an empirical issue. Is it possible to find historical patterns in the time series that can be used for at least rough predictions of the future price?

The German tradition can get some support from the American professor Richard Ratcliff who wrote several leading textbooks on property valuations in the 1960s (e.g. Ratcliff 1972). He pointed out that valuation for lending purposes must discuss how much the property will be worth at a future point in time when the borrower might have economic difficulties and must sell the property. This future price will affect the profitability of the loan and then it should be rational for a bank to try to estimate this future price: see the next chapter for further discussions.

4.6 Client Influence and Bias

Uncertainty and limited evidence can lead to biased valuations as it opens the door to client influence (see, e.g. Levy and Schuck 1999, 2005; Crosby et al. 2010). Client influence can occur also in a world of certainty, but then it is more like fraud, but here the focus is on bias that can occur when there is uncertainty. In an accounting context, the same phenomenon is discussed under the heading 'management bias' and will be discussed further in Chapter 6 (Selling and Nordlund 2015).[2]

The valuer is to a considerable extent dependent on information from the property owner. This concerns both physical data (e.g. areas), economic data (e.g. net operating income) and legal information (e.g. contracts). In some cases, the valuer takes this information for granted and makes a *conditional valuation*. The valuation report estimates the market value, *given* that the information provided by the property owner is correct. If this information is biased, then the resulting valuation will be biased, but in this situation, the valuer has done nothing wrong.

---

2 McAllister (2020) describes that also how brokers behave can lead to bias in the market, which then feeds into property valuations.

It is clear from the valuation report that it is based on information from the owner and that these data have not been checked by the valuer.

The valuer may also be excused if there is a more sophisticated fraud by the owner, e.g. presenting false data and false documents that look correct. The valuer makes the normal checks of the information provided by the owner and truly believes that the data are correct, but the result will still be a biased valuation.

The bias in the valuation may, however, not be related to the information used but occur in the analysis and conclusion stage. Bias may occur in this stage as there are subjective elements, e.g. when deciding the weight that should be given to a specific comparable sale or when deciding the adjustments that are needed for the remaining differences between valuation object and the comparative sales. Klamer et al. (2019), for example, show that client attachment can lead to a situation where the valuer puts less effort into verification of data. If the true market value is 100, there is little risk of saying that the market value is 105. Some valuers may say that they are a little more optimistic about the market than other valuers and argue that there exist potential buyers who share this optimism. Bias in the direction wanted by the client would then be rather risk free as long as the difference between the estimated market value and the true market value is in the range 5–10% - it would then be within the margin of error discussed above.

More theoretically, the valuer can be seen as a utility maximizing agent in a world where some clients prefer a higher or lower value compared to the true market value. A client that wants to borrow money may want to have a high value to make a larger loan possible. In other cases, a lower value may be preferred, as a future increase in value then is more probable and that may be preferable if, for example, a bonus is linked to the value increases (see Baum et al. 2000). A bias in the direction that the client wants can lead to more work and higher income in the future, but there is also a risk of getting a bad reputation. The bad reputation can also lead to loss of work as the values presented by this person will not be seen as credible by users of the valuation. The larger the uncertainty in the estimation of the market value, the lower should the risk be in supplying a somewhat biased valuation. As will be returned to in Chapter 9, how an authorization agency acts will also affect the cost for the valuer if supplying a biased valuation.

From a general perspective, the tendency to fall for the temptations to supply a biased valuation can be expected to increase if the valuer, or the valuation company, has economic problems. Being on the verge of bankruptcy changes incentives and what appears irrational when a company is doing well can be rational if the company or the valuer have economic problems. There are also psychological mechanisms that can make it easier to supply a biased valuation. Psychologists have observed 'self-serving bias' in peoples' beliefs, which means that people have a tendency to believe what is in their interest to believe. This means that the valuer might not see the biased valuation as biased. A biased valuation can also be rationalized by a belief that if I do not present a biased valuation, then someone else will. The only difference is who gets the money.

In different contexts, there has been a call for discussions about the need for more rigorous monitoring, surveillance and possible disciplinary actions when it comes to the work of valuers. Is there a need for stronger mechanisms or institutions for this? Client pressure is one of the reasons behind such proposals. This is discussed more in detail in Chapter 9.

4.7 Behavioural Factors

During the last decades, behavioural theories have grown in importance in economics. Important names are, for example, Nobel Prize winners Daniel Kahneman and Richard Thaler. These theories can be defined in relation to standard microeconomic theory where a number of assumptions are made about how a rational person acts. The starting point for the behavioural theories was a number of experiments that indicated that people did not act in a way that was consistent with standard microeconomic theory and with the expected-utility theory about behaviour under uncertainty. The behavioural studies show that persons can act in a way that leads to systematic bias in relation to how a rational person would behave.

There have been a large number of behavioural studies of the real estate market and the behaviour of property valuers. An early survey can be found in Diaz (1999) and a more recent one in Salzman and Zwinkels (2017). Studies of the real estate market have, for example, found that investors might be *irrationally optimistic* and be *overconfident* concerning their possibility to handle different future problems. They may also be affected by *herd-behaviour.* Investors also use various simplifying *heuristics* (rules of thumb) and rely on intuition or 'gut feelings' when they make investments. As described in Chapter 2, there might be *loss aversion,* which means that an owner might postpone a planned selling because they do not want to sell at a price that is lower than what they bought the property for, or lower than the value in the financial reports. A general tendency is also *confirmation bias,* that most people look for information that confirms their beliefs and tend to disregard, or at least give lower weight to, information that points in other directions.

Julian Diaz III and Andrew Hansz have in a number of publications applied and developed these theories in the area of property valuation (e.g. Hansz 2004; Diaz and Hansz 2010). A number of behavioural patterns have been identified, but here the focus will be on two such patterns: Herd behaviour, and Anchoring and adjustment.

Herd behaviour means that people tend to shift their views or actions so they come closer to what they think others believe, or what they think other people will do. If the information that a valuer has at hand points to a market value of 100, but that the valuer believes that other valuers will put a value of 110 on that type of property, then the valuer may choose to conclude that the market value is 105. Herd behaviour can be interpreted in terms of risk-averseness. If it turns out that the transacted price is close to the result of the other's valuations, it may affect your reputation if your valuation is too far from what others have said. It is less risky to join the herd, or at least stay close to the herd. This tendency might be stronger for younger and less experienced valuers. These arguments also imply that it can be rational for an individual to act in this way and shift their views closer to the average. Behavioural factors are not necessarily a sign of irrationality, even if it might be in conflict with the basic assumptions in standard microeconomic theory where an individual's behaviour only is determined by their own information and their own preferences over their own consumption bundles.

Anchoring and adjustment. Another pattern found in several experiments is that a valuer starts from certain information (the anchor), e.g. a recent assessed value, a recently contracted price, a recent valuation of the property or a desired loan amount. Then the valuer adjusts the value in relation to this anchor, based on recent information of different types, but the choice of anchor will still affect the final result. An implication of this theory is that different valuers might reach different results as they might have started from different anchors. Baum et al. (2000, p. 13) write:

> Research into how valuers undertake their task has revealed that they do not necessarily follow expected procedures nor use information in the ways generally assumed. As indicated above, valuers are prone to display 'biases' in arriving at their judgements. Most typical of these biases is 'anchoring'. Anchoring is a form of behaviour in which people, when required to arrive at an estimate, do so by adjusting from an initial starting figure.

The results of such a study are presented in Amidu et al. (2019a, b) and they underline the role that intuition plays in the valuation process. A recent study also indicates that different anchors lead to different values even if the persons carrying out the valuation have been educated about possible anchoring effects (Palm and Andersson 2020). A critical evaluation of the literature about judgement bias can be found in Klamer et al. (2017).

Another interesting result from Kahneman is that people tend to give new information greater weight than is rational. If this is true for valuers, it should imply that valuations fluctuate more than the underlying true values. On the other hand, a risk-averse valuer that anchors a new valuation in a recently done valuation may hesitate to make larger adjustments and will therefore instead make valuations that fluctuate less than the underlying true market value. This leads to another issue discussed in the literature: valuation smoothing – see the next section.

Behavioural aspects have also been discussed in the context of auditing fair (market) values (e.g. Martin et al. 2006). The auditor needs to be aware of several of the mechanisms discussed above, especially the following two. Overconfidence and information quality: There is a risk that access to large quantities of information may lead to management's overconfidence in making fair (market) value-assessments. Confirmation bias: There is a tendency to search for information that supports previously held beliefs regarding, for instance, the level of future cash flows applied in a fair (market) value assessment model.

4.8 Valuation Smoothing

As mentioned in Section 4.1, there have been arguments that valuation both lag the development on the market and also smooth the development in the sense that cycles in values are smaller than cycles in the underlying prices. The background to this discussion is that investors want to be able to compare risk and return from different asset classes. In order to do that, they need indices describing the return and risk for different asset classes. As the number of transactions on the real estate market is relatively small, indices for real estate are often constructed from valuations and not from actual transactions. The literature about valuation smoothing started from the observation that using valuations can lead to an underestimation of the variance of the returns (see, e.g. Geltner et al. 2003). As valuations also take into account earlier transactions and not only the most recent ones, the result would be that valuations lead to a smoother index. The real estate index may therefore overestimate the attractiveness of real estate compared to other asset classes as risk would be underestimated.

It is, however, important to understand that using older transactions does not necessarily mean that the specific valuation is biased, even if it leads to a smoother index. In an important article, Quan and Quigley (1991) argue that using older transactions can be rational in a situation where there are few transactions in each time period and large random variations in each observation. The ideas presented in that article can be seen as an application of a more general Bayesian updating rule. In Bayesian updating, one starts with a 'prior' – e.g. a view about the most probable price – and then this prior is updated using new information and the result is a 'posterior' probability. How much the probability should change depends on how probable the new information is given various hypotheses. If there are large random variations in price, then observing a new transaction with a higher or lower price will not motivate a large change in the probability of a certain price. If the random variation is low, then observing a price that differs from the earlier market value is a strong argument for at least making some adjustments in the estimated market value.

Quan and Quigley (1991) formulate their conclusion as follows:

> The key to the model is the updating rule which the appraiser employs to extract the price signal from 'noisy' transactions made by imperfectly informed actors in the market. This rule specifies the appropriate weighting of the information in a given transaction with the stock of prior information available to the appraiser. This stock of information is the experience and human capital of the appraiser, which forms the basis for signal extraction. (p. 141)
>
> if the variability of prices due to conditions of sale is large relative to the marketwide noise, then appraisers will rely more heavily in the previous estimate, rather than on the most recently observed transaction price. (p. 141)

If using older information leads to the best possible estimation of the market value, it is not really clear what is meant by saying that the market value lags the development of the market and smooth the development of returns. These formulations indicate that there is a 'true' value that is higher (or lower) than the estimated market value and a development of 'true' values that is not as smooth as the development of the estimated market values. But these true values are impossible to know – and then claims about lags and smoothing are not verifiable. In the theoretical articles, it is often assumed that there is an underlying distribution of prices and that observed prices are 'drawn' from this distribution. The result will then depend on assumptions about this underlying distribution – assumption that cannot be verified either. Problems related to index construction will not be discussed further here, but the interested reader is recommended to look at the real estate finance literature.

It should finally be noted that there are conflicting tendencies in the more theoretical debates. The literature on lags and smoothing argue that too little weight is given to more recent information, while the behavioural literature argues that too much weight is given to more recent information (availability bias).

4.9 How Self-Selection Can Lead to 'Bias'

It is, as noted in the last section, not always clear what should be seen as bias and what should not. The following example can illustrate another problem of this kind. Let us first assume that a random selection of similar properties is sold each period. Single-family houses might, for example, be sold when the owner dies and the probability of death is at least in general independent of external factors like the business cycle. From observed data for these transactions, a market value is estimated and would give the best prediction of what the price would be if a random property of this type was sold.

But suppose that in period 1 a market value of 100 is estimated and that whether a property will be sold in period 2 is determined by the company owning the property. The company has a general policy saying that they should sell only if they can report a profit, i.e. they are more likely to sell if the current price is higher than the last valuation.

Suppose furthermore that there are some differences in characteristics, and somewhat different locations, between the properties that still are seen as belonging to the same market in the city. The demand for these different types of properties changes somewhat between period 1 and period 2, with increasing demand for some and decreasing demand for others. If a random selection of properties were sold - or at least the same selection as last year - the market value is assumed to be 100 also in period 2, as the value would be 95 in the declining part and 105 in the part of the market where prices have increased. As companies with the policy mentioned above will sell more often if they own a property where demand has increased, they are assumed to sell only in the part of the market where prices have increased to 105. A market value based on these transactions will then be 105, and it would appear that market values had increased to 105.

Shall we say that this estimated market value is biased or not? It is not biased in the sense that it actually gives a correct market value if you sell properties with the characteristic that the sold properties have. But if the higher market value in period 2 is interpreted as information about the market as a whole, it is biased upwards as the composition of the transacted properties have changed and that the higher prices in period 2 only reflect this change in composition of the transacted properties in relation to the average property on the specific market.

In our view, the main conclusion from this is that when there are changes in average prices observed, one must always check carefully if the composition of properties have changed and if there are underlying patterns where changes in demand affect the probability of a transaction. This problem is related to the discussion about turnover in Chapter 2, where a fall in demand can lead to lower turnover but the same price, even if this high price only is possible for a small number of transactions. In both cases, it can be risky to draw conclusions from observed prices to probable price if another object is sold. When housing price indices are constructed (see, e.g. Song and Wilhelmsson 2010), changes in the characteristics of the properties sold between periods are controlled for by using a hedonic method. This would not work on the commercial market since there are too few transactions in relation to the number of dimensions where properties might differ.

Another obvious problem is when a company (X) holding property A and property B have got, for example, an estimated market value of 100 on A and 100 on B and in the next step finds out that actors in the market are willing to pay say 115 for A but only 85 for B. Probably, if not very eager to sell, company X will sell property A but not property B. Hence, information from the transaction market is 'selected' from company X perspective. The willingness to pay 'only' 85 for property B may not be visible on the market.

4.10 Possible Policy Recommendations

As mentioned in Section 4.1, discussions about uncertainty in property valuations and how they can be reported typically intensify after a crash on the real estate markets. An example is Mallinson and French (1999) that discuss the idea that a probability distribution for the value should be presented, and not just a single figure. Such a probability distribution can, however, be interpreted in two different ways and from the article it is not clear which one is intended:

1) A probability distribution of *prices* for a specific property. How probable is it that you will get a price close to the market value? In Table 4.2, it is more probable that you will get a price close to the market value in the first case compared to the second case, as the distribution of observed prices is less dispersed in that case.

2) A probability distribution for the *market value*. How probable is it that the presented market value really is the most probable price? In the cases presented in Table 4.2, it is in both cases rather sure what the probable price is, even though the probability of getting a price close to the market value differs. In general, the distribution of the market value is narrower than the distribution of prices.

A simple and rather common way to present uncertainty concerning the market value is to present an *interval* for the market value, e.g. that the market value is A ± 5% or A ± 10%. Ekelid et al. (1998) show that this practice increased in Sweden after the real estate crash in the early 1990s.

A problem is how such an interval should be interpreted: With what probability is the market value (or the price) within this interval? Typically, nothing is said about that. And if the same interval is used in all valuations, there is no information about how uncertain a specific valuation is, even though some valuations should be more certain than others. RICS (2012, p. 117)[3] also argues against presenting an interval for the value.

---

3 This is from the guidance note VPGA 10 Matters that may give rise to material valuation uncertainty.

One method discussed in a number of articles, e.g. Lorenz et al. (2006), is to use Monte Carlo simulations. Especially, if a discounted cash flow method is used, assumptions about all the input variables can be changed and new values calculated. By making assumptions about the probability distribution of all input variables, and then letting a computer make a large number of random draws, a probability distribution for the market value can be derived.

There are problems also with this approach, e.g. how should one choose the underlying distribution of the input variables, and what assumptions should be made about independence between these assumptions? This means that in the end it is difficult to know how probable the derived probability distribution really is. RICS (2012, p. 117) writes:

> If a mathematical measure of uncertainty is included in any report, it is essential that the method or model used is adequately explained, with any limitations appropriately highlighted. In some limited circumstances a sensitivity analysis may be judged appropriate in order to illustrate the effect that clearly stated changes to specified variables could have on the reported *valuation*, which should be accompanied by suitable explanatory comment. It will be appreciated that the inherent risk with quantification of any sort is that it might convey an impression of precision that could be misleading.

Aristotle wrote that it is a sign of wise person that they do not try to reach a higher degree of certainty than the nature of the subject allows. Things can, for example, be proved in mathematics but not in ethics. Given the heterogeneity of real estate objects, the small number of transactions and the rate of changes in an economy, it might not be fruitful to try to make a quantitative estimation of how uncertain a certain valuation is. A more qualitative presentation of uncertainty might be better, and such a presentation could, for example, include:

1) *What type of information is used in the valuation.* The fair value hierarchy presented in Chapter 2 can be used for this. Have comparative sales been available? Is the valuation based on more general knowledge of how the actors in the market think and calculate?
2) *The strength of the evidence.* Does the collected information points very clearly in a certain direction? Should one expect to get a price close to this market value or does the information instead point to a rather large interval where the price might end up?
3) A more general comment on *the relative certainty of this specific valuation compared to other valuations of similar properties.* Is this specific valuation relatively more or less uncertain compared to other valuations of this type of property on this type of market?

If and how information about the stability of the market value in the future should be presented is discussed further in the next chapter about valuation for lending purposes.

A more explicit discussion of uncertainty and the evidence for the proposed market value could in itself be important for reducing bias. In the field of accounting and auditing, a number of measures have over the years been proposed to weaken the influence of the client, e.g. that the client has to change audit firm after some years. These issues will be returned to in Chapters 8 and 9 about transparency and governance.

4.11   Concluding Comments

Reid (2016) and Walvekar and Kakka (2020) compare valuations and transaction prices from a number of countries. The first observation in these studies is that transaction prices on average are around 4–5% higher than a recent valuation of that property. A second observation is that the gap between valuations and observed prices are cyclical. The gap is high in the boom and almost not existent during a serious downturn in the market.

Given the arguments presented in this chapter, these observations can have the following explanations:

1) *Incentives*: Maybe property owners/managers prefer a somewhat lower value so they can sell with a reported profit. Smaller increases in values over several years might be better for them than one large increase in value during a boom, perhaps followed by a small reported fall in values when the cycles turn down. Then, it is rational to undervalue during periods where the market goes up.

2) *Anchoring and adjustment combined with risk aversion*: If the valuer anchors the value in earlier valuations and are risk averse, the result will be that when the market goes up, the valuer may lag the market. If the value of the properties has not increased so much during the upturn, then when the valuer starts to reduce the value in small steps during the downturn, the valuer may end up with the correct value when the market hits the bottom. It might also be riskier for the valuer to overestimate the value, as they might be criticized by investors who bought at the high prices.

3) *Self-selection*: Properties are perhaps primarily sold when it is possible to report a profit. During the boom there will be optimistic actors who are willing to pay more than the estimated market value. When the market turns down and hits the bottom, these actors disappear. If the current actors are not willing to sell below the estimated market value, the result will be prices close to the market value during the recession.

Exercises

1   Interview both clients and valuers in your local market about their views on how uncertain valuations are? How does the uncertainty about values vary, e.g. with type of property and location?

2   Does banks trust valuations that a property owner presents? Do they want to make their own valuation? Are they afraid that there might be client bias in the valuations?

3   Do bank and buyers of valuations have the same degree of confidence in the estimates made by different valuers (valuation companies) or do they know some valuers as prudent and others as optimistic?

4   As mentioned in the text, property valuations often come under scrutiny after a crash on the market. Is that true also in your local market?

5   What are your views on quantitative versus qualitative presentations of uncertainty?

6   Pro or con: Should the valuer also discuss stability of the value over time, and rate the risk for falling prices for the specific property?

5

Valuation for Lending Purposes and Long-Term Value Concepts

5.1 Introduction

One of the most important purposes of property valuation is as a foundation for lending decisions in the banking sector. The interest in the role of valuation for lending purposes is also related to the role of credit in the real estate cycle. Excessive lending by banks with property as collateral has by some researchers been seen as one of the most important causes of price bubbles and financial crises. This also means that changes related to property valuations can affect the risk for future crises. Crosby and Hughes (2011) discuss 'whether reconsidering the basis of valuation of commercial real estate can play a part in preventing future havoc' (p. 255).[1]

As the market value gives a snapshot of the current market while a lender should think about the value of the property at a future point in time when the borrower might have economic problems, it is obvious that looking only at the current market value might be problematic, something already noted by Ratcliff (1972). In such a situation, it is natural to look for alternative value concepts that in one way or the other tries to capture more of a long-run perspective.

This interest in a more long-term value also means that theories about the predictability of property prices, and theories about price bubbles, are highly relevant in the context of valuation for lending decisions. These issues are discussed in Sections 5.2 and 5.3. As cycles in property price can be related to how banks behave in different phases of a business cycle, theories of banking behaviour must also be covered (Section 5.4). The idea that some kind of risk-analysis can be made to evaluate how likely it is that prices will fall is discussed in Section 5.5. After the discussion of these more fundamental issues, four general strategies concerning lending and the business cycles are discussed: (1) using only the current market value but

---

1 See also RICS (2018), p. 2.

Advanced Issues in Property Valuation, First Edition. Hans Lind and Bo Nordlund.
© 2021 John Wiley & Sons Ltd. Published 2021 by John Wiley & Sons Ltd.

make adjustment in the loan-to-value (LTV) ratios, (2) using different value concepts like mortgage lending value and (3) using some derivative of market value, e.g. a moving average, or (4) using some kind of cost-based value. One can see all these strategies as ways of reducing the risk of lending too much to property during a boom in the economy. After the discussion of these different strategies in Sections 5.6–5.10, some concluding comments can be found in Section 5.11.

In *The Appraisal of Real Estate* (2013), there are no specific discussions about value concepts and methods for lending purpose or about valuation problems linked to the property cycle. The same holds for Wyatt (2013) and IVSC (2019). RICS has issued a special guidance note on valuation for secured lending that is also included in RICS (2018). In that guidance note, they also discuss the concept of mortgage lending value that will be covered in Section 5.7.

5.2 Two Competing Theories About Predictability of Property Prices

As discussed in the last chapter, the efficient market hypothesis says in its simplest form that current asset prices reflect all available information and the best theories available, and that prices therefore are unpredictable (follow a 'random walk'). If there are new information about, say, the future economic situation or future policies, real estate prices will change immediately. An example can be that there is new macroeconomic information, e.g. about an unexpected increase or reduction of incoming orders to industry or that the central bank publishes a new unexpected prediction of their future interest rates. All such news changes expectations on the market. On the housing market, it is often easy to see that changes in current or expected central bank interest rates directly affect house prices, especially in countries where many have loans with variable interest rates.

If prices only change when there is new unexpected information, then it is not possible to predict the future level of asset prices, as new unexpected information per definition cannot be predicted. This means that it is impossible to claim that current prices are too high or too low, or that we are in a certain stage of a property cycle where there soon will be a turning point for the better or for worse. At any point of time, it is just as likely that the price level will go up as it is that it will go down. This theory is supported both by so-called event studies showing that asset prices quickly react to new conditions and by more common-sense arguments. If prices were predictable, it would be easy to make a lot of money by using this information, e.g. by various types of future contracts. Eugene Fama got the Nobel Prize in Economics for his role in developing and testing this theory and in his Nobel lecture, he presents the theory and the studies that support it (Fama 2014).

It should be mentioned that the theory only implies that the price for a building with certain given characteristic is unpredictable. As a building ages, its quality falls and it is of course possible to predict that the relative value of the property will fall over time if no investments are made in the property. But if it is common knowledge that the quality falls, the information about falling values cannot be used to make profitable investments.

Fama shared the Nobel Prize with Robert Shiller, who questioned the efficient market theory (see, e.g. Shiller 2014). Shiller found in his empirical studies that asset prices show 'mean reversion', i.e. a fall in price is more likely after a period of rising prices and that an increase in prices are more likely after a series of falling prices. This is just another way of saying that the data indicate that asset prices are cyclical, even if the theory does not imply that cycles are regular or predictable in length and magnitude. Shiller also questions the argument that predictability would cause risk-free profit opportunities. Imagine that the economy is in a recession and that property prices have fallen. If there is a property cycle, it should be expected that prices soon will rise. But if it is not known when and with how much prices will rise, it will be risky to speculate in increasing property prices. There might be large initial losses and risk of bankruptcy before the 'certain' profits occur. Especially if investments are evaluated over a short-time period, fund managers might not be willing to take the risk of speculating in increasing asset prices during a recession, or speculate in falling prices during a boom.[2]

5.3 Price Bubbles on the Real Estate Market

Property cycles or – more generally – asset price cycles can be more or less dramatic. Especially, dramatic fluctuations have been called asset price bubbles. Garber (2000) describes and discusses a number of classic historical price bubbles. During the Tulipmania in Holland 1636–1637, the prices of tulip bulbs at the peak were 100 times the prices both before and after.

The most common definition of an asset price bubble is the one presented by Stiglitz (1990):

> if the reason that the price is high today is only because investors believe that the selling price will be high tomorrow – when 'fundamental' factors do not seem to justify such a price – then a bubble exist.
>
> *(Stiglitz 1990, p. 13)*

---

2 We recommend the movie 'The big short' (2015) for an illustration of both the risks and the possible gains in speculating in future property prices.

What is counted as fundamental factors is explained in the following way:

> The problem of determining the fundamental value of an asset to be held for an extended period of time has three parts: first, the problem of estimating the returns received over time (the rent on the land, the dividends on the stock); second, the problem of estimating the terminal value the asset will have at the end of the period; and third, the problem of deciding upon the discount rates to be used for translating future returns into current values.

In the context of property valuation, this means that whether there is a bubble or not on the commercial real estate market can be evaluated by comparing the current prices with investment values calculated in a 'rational' way. This idea is developed in an article by Crosby and Hughes (2011) that we will return to below.

For the apartment and housing market, the fundamentals can be seen as the factors that determine such prices on a rational market. In the short run, typical fundamentals are then incomes, interest rates and financing possibilities, operating costs and cost for alternative housing (rent levels). As indicated by the cost approach to valuation, in the long term, the price level will also be affected by the cost of increasing the housing stock.

Lind (2009) describes three different mechanisms that can lead to prices above the level that is motivated by fundamentals. The first is a pure speculative bubble, where buyers pay a price that they know is irrationally high, because they expect to be able to sell at an even higher price before the bubble bursts. This mechanism is more likely on the stock market where transaction costs are low. On the real estate market with higher transaction cost and longer transaction processes, this strategy is much riskier.

The second mechanism is based on the hypothesis that the actors on the market can show what Shiller (2000) calls 'irrational exuberance', or more generally: that buyers pay too much because they have irrational positive expectations about the future. After the Swedish real estate and banking crisis in the early 1990, one bank manager commented that 'somewhere along the way we lost contact with reality'. Glaeser (2013) points to underestimation of future supply increases as another example where irrational expectations can lead to price bubbles.

The third mechanism is where people pay too high prices because they believe that they will be able to get a share of a potential gain but be able to shift eventual losses to someone else. This is a classical moral hazard problem that has been discussed much. Banks and other big financial institutions may be 'too big to fail' and take too much risk because they expect to be saved by the government if they have serious economic problems. Lind (2009) calls this a bubble caused by irrational institutions, and Glaeser (2013) explains a similar mechanism in terms of 'mis-priced default option': if the institutions default, then they will be able to shift losses to someone else and default is therefore too cheap.

There is a major problem with the concept of price bubbles and that is that economists never seem to agree whether there is a bubble or not on a specific market during a certain period of time. This is caused by problems in the concept of fundamentals and in knowing what is rational to expect concerning, for example, future values of the net operating income and future interest rates. House prices increased considerably during the last decade in a number of countries (see Knoll et al. 2017). It could be argued that this is a bubble, as prices have increased more than incomes and production costs. It could also be argued that the higher prices are rational given lower interest rate (both short term and long term) and as there are restrictions on increasing supply in a number of regions. The question of whether there is a bubble or not then boils down to the questions whether it is rational to believe that interest rates will be low for a long time, and if it is rational to believe that the increase in the supply of cheaper houses will be low. And it is of course difficult to know what will happen to interest rates or supply in say 5–10 years!

In the rest of this book, we will not use the concept of price bubble, but it is of course still important to try to analyse whether property prices are likely to fall or not. One way to approach this issue is through risk analysis that will be discussed in Section 5.5.

5.4 The Leverage Cycles and Bank Incentives

Another important background factor to rules about valuation and lending is the behaviour of banks over the business cycle. It might be assumed that banks are rational and use all available information to evaluate property prices and their probable future development when they determine acceptable LTV ratios. The competing theories about asset price predictability presented above have different implications for how a rational bank would set the LTV-ratio. As the efficient market theory implies that prices are unpredictable, there would be no reason for banks to change the LTV-ratio when prices are going up or down. Even if prices have risen, the prices might just as well continue to go up or fall, and there would be no reason to reduce the LTV-ratios when prices have risen. We should therefore expect a constant LTV-ratio over the business cycle. This LTV-ratio would be based on an analysis of the volatility of prices and the risk that the bank is willing to take.

If there is mean reversion and property cycles, the rational strategy for a bank would be to reduce the LTV-ratios when prices have increased, as the probability of a fall in prices is higher in the boom. For the same reason, the rational bank would increase the LTV-ratio when prices have fallen, as an increase in prices then is more likely and a higher LTV-ratio would not be so risky.

Empirical studies of bank behaviour, however, indicate that there is a procyclical leverage cycle and more generous lending when there is a boom in the economy and when property prices have risen. The economist John Geanakoplos has in a series of papers discussed the 'leverage cycle', e.g. in Geanakoplos (2010). This literature shows that banks typically do not follow either of the patterns above. Instead, the LTV-ratios increase during a boom period. This means that lending becomes more generous in the boom, which can lead to even higher prices. A price increase is seen as a signal that prices will continue to increase even more, and such expectations would make an increased LTV-ratio rational.

There are several possible explanations for such a leverage cycle. The banks may in the boom also be characterized by 'irrational exuberance'. Competition between banks has also been pointed out as a contributing factor, where banks are afraid of losing business opportunities to competitors if they do not become more generous in their lending. Moral hazard problems in banks can also lead to too much and too risky lending (see e.g. Cole and Eisenbeis 1996). The effect of these mechanisms may be a spiral where increased lending leads to higher prices which rationalize a continued increase in lending. There are stories from insiders that during the Swedish real estate boom in the late 1980s, it was possible to borrow more than the current market value when a property was bought – as the bank argued that prices were rising quickly and that therefore the value of the property soon would be higher than the loan amount. A high general inflation also contributed to this, but the high lending levels soon turned out to be unsustainable when the market dipped.

A crisis on the real estate market, and a questioning of the rationality of the banking sector, typically leads to discussion about whether there need to be stricter rules for banks concerning, for example, collateral and reserves. Such demands are also logical given the theories that excessive lending that leads to price bubbles and increased risks for financial instability.

5.5 Use Market Value, Make Risk Analysis and Adjust the Loan-to-Value Ratio (LTV-Ratio)

Wyatt (2013, p. 280) notes that market value is the dominating value concept for lending purposes (p. 280) - in Anglo-Saxon countries, he could have added. Risks of different kinds are then handled in the determination of LTV-ratio. In their critique of the concept mortgage lending value - see below - Crosby et al. (2000) argue for such a strategy, even if they also discuss the concept of worth which will be returned to below.

A bank, or a regulator, that believes in rather regular business cycles should, as argued above, reduce the LTV-ratio when financing a transaction if there has been strong growth in market values for a number of years and then increase LTV-ratio when property values have fallen. Such a strategy will also tend to stabilize property values as lending becomes more restrictive during the boom. If future prices are judged to be impossible to predict, a rational bank or a regulator that wants to reduce the risk of bank failures if prices fall would then set a relatively low but constant LTV-ratio, e.g. a maximum of 70% for a new mortgage. The exact level of the ratio could be based on historical data about how probable price falls of a certain magnitude have been, and on an evaluation of how a situation with larger price falls could be handled.

In the academic literature, there are also a number of articles, especially from German researchers about how such risk analysis related to probable future prices could be carried out. A version of such an analysis can, as mentioned earlier, be found in Lorenz et al. (2006). This concerns the type of uncertainty that in Chapter 4 was discussed under the heading 'uncertainty about the future market value'. It should, however, be noted that this kind of analysis hardly is possible if the efficient market hypothesis is correct. Our recommendation when there are competing theories is that a practitioner must analyse the situation using both theories, and if the efficient market theory does not hold, then it is meaningful to make a risk analysis.

The risk analysis presented in the above-mentioned article discusses a large number of risks on different levels, but here the focus will be on a few more general risks that should be relevant from the perspective of valuation for lending purposes. The selection and comments are ours and should only be seen as examples of how one could argue.

5.5.1 Risk Related to the National Economic Situation and the Capital Market

If e.g. GDP and property prices have risen strongly for several years, the risk for a downturn in the economy might be higher. The development of property prices is also related to the developments in the capital market. If there has been either generous lending or a large inflow of capital from investment funds to the property market, then it could be argued that such policies cannot go on forever and that the risks for more restricted capital flows and falling property prices are higher.

Macroeconomic policies should also be taken into account. During a recession, the net operating income and expected future net operating income typically fall, but how property values react depends on what happens to the rate of return demanded. Sweden is a good illustration of how different macroeconomic regimes can affect the development of property values. In the economic downturn during the early 1990s, Sweden had a fixed exchange rate and the central bank increased the interest rate to defend the value of the currency. For a short period of time, the central bank interest rate was as high as 500%. As investors after the crash realized that real estate was riskier than they had thought, both the 'safe' interest rate and the risk adjustment were increased with a dramatic fall in property prices as a result. When the financial crisis hit Sweden in the summer of 2008, the country had floating exchange rates and the central bank was free to reduce the interest rate to stimulate the economy. The drastic fall in the 'safe' interest rate meant that the rate of return demanded also fell which stabilized the price level on the commercial real estate market. The falling interest rates also helped the cash flow of the companies and reduced the number of forced sales which also contributed to stabilizing the property prices.

Institutional conditions might also affect the risk for falling prices. It is, for example, argued in Crosby et al. (2010) that the large fall in prices for commercial properties in the United Kingdom during the latest financial crisis was related to certain types of investment funds for which it was better with a large quick fall than a slower and more drawn-out development. In that way they could avoid a run on the fund.

5.5.2 Risk Related to the Local Economic Situation

A specific location, in a country, region or city, may also be judged to be more or less risky and be affected by different types of trends. A certain area in a city may, for example, become more or less attractive when there are changes in the communication networks or just changes in preferences and in the status of different areas. More random factors, e.g. a new production facility – or the closing of an old production facility – may affect the attractiveness of a certain location.

5.5.3 Risk Related to Climate Change

More or less dramatic changes can be expected on all property markets related to climate change. This can be related to both long-term changes in sea levels and to increasing risk for extreme weather conditions with flooding and very strong winds that can damage the building. According to our information, banks are already developing systems to evaluate these risks and some lenders are, for example, becoming more sceptical to properties that are located in areas with higher flooding risks. This will be discussed more in Chapter 7.

5.5.4 Risk Related to Specific Characteristics of the Property

Another aspect that also will be discussed more in Chapter 7 is risk related to 'brown' buildings with a large environmental impact. Future regulations might reduce the value of such buildings. The risk of investing in a specific building may also be related to how flexible the building is. An example is that there have been changes in the demand for offices where the demand has fallen for old-fashioned offices with single rooms but increased for offices with more open spaces. From an investor perspective, it might then be riskier to invest in an old-fashioned office building that is difficult to transform into a modern office building.

5.5.5 But Are These Risks Already Capitalized into the Price?

A risk analysis of some type can lead to a classification of buildings into more or less risky from the perspective of the future development of the value of the building. The classification can then be used when decisions about lending are made, e.g. a lower LTV-ratio or a higher interest rate for the riskier building. One has, however, to take into account the possibility that these risks already have affected prices and that the risk for falling prices is not so high after all. Once again, we come back to the conflict between the efficient market theory and theories that say that maybe the actors are not so rational after all. Maybe current prices do not reflect the best theories and all available information.

5.6 'Long-Run Value' as an Alternative

The strategy that seems to be the dominating one in Anglo-saxon countries is that banks start from the current market value and then use other information, e.g. about the risks discussed above, to set the LTV-ratio and the interest rate. An alternative – or complementary – strategy is the use of other value concepts than market value when lending decisions are made. In different documents from RICS, a 'long-term value' is discussed.

In RICS (2017, p. 30), the following can be read:

> There is no doubt that market value will remain the main valuation base for many purposes. But at the same time, clients are increasingly asking for 'long-term value'. Different terms are used, such as long-term value, (real) economic value, sustainable value and the already existing mortgage lending value. However, until now it has never been fully developed. Clients know why they want 'long-term value', but not necessarily what it looks like.

RICS (2018, p. 10) notes that 'a variety of other stakeholders in real estate finance are investigating other long-term value concepts as part of the post-GFC financial stability agenda'. In Burston and Burrell (2015), two such concepts are discussed, one based on historical patterns of earnings and one based on comparison with other assets.

This is not the first time in history such value concepts have been brought forward. Lind and Persson (1998) discuss the background to and the need for value concepts other than market value. They underline that the demand for a long-term value typically arise after a crash on the real estate market, e.g. in the 1930s and in the 1990s, when the focus on current market value was questioned.

A common feature of many of these alternative value concepts is that they can be seen as a *hypothetical market value*, e.g. what the market value would be if the actors are rational or what the market value would be if there is a 'normal' situation in the economy and on the real estate market. A common problem with many of these alternative value concepts is that they are vague and in practice difficult to be estimated in a reasonably objective way. This will be illustrated in the coming sections where more specific versions of long-term values are analysed.

5.7   Alternative Value Concept (1) Mortgage Lending Value

The most important alternative value concept in the context of bank lending is the Mortgage lending value (MLV) that is defined in the following way:

> (Regulation (EU) No 575/2013, article 4 (74) 'mortgage lending value' means the value of immovable property as determined by a prudent assessment of the future marketability of the property taking into account long-term sustainable aspects of the property, the normal and local market conditions, the current use and alternative appropriate uses of the property.)
> *Taken from http://www.rics.org/se/news/news-insight/news/ mortgage-lending-value-in-the-eu/.*

The underlying argument is that the market value fluctuates (too much) with the business cycle. If the banks are assumed to apply the same LTV over the business cycle, there is a risk that lending might be too high in the boom with a possible banking crisis when property values fall in the recession. This risk is even higher if banks have a procyclical variation in the LTV-ratio as discussed in the previous section about the leverage cycle.

If the definition of MLV is evaluated from the perspectives of clarity and the possibility of objective application, it is a very problematic definition (see, e.g.

Crosby et al. 2000). What is meant with 'a prudent assessment', 'future marketability', 'long-term sustainable aspects' and 'normal market conditions'?

Bienert and Brunauer (2007) discuss the concept of MLV more in detail and identify two different interpretations. In the first interpretation, the MLV is derived from the market value, and in the second interpretation, the MLV is calculated in a separate way from how the market value is calculated. In the article, it is said that only the second method is judged to be acceptable, and the focus in their article is therefore on that strategy.[3] Derivatives of market value are discussed in Section 5.8. Bienert and Brunauer (2007) also note:

> In fact it is the job of the valuer to inform the lender about the potential future direction of the MV during the loan period, otherwise the bank is not in the position to decide today whether the loan amount relative to the MV is acceptable or not. (p. 552)

The method to calculate the MLV is in Germany strictly regulated by the authorities. A cost-based or an income-based approach should be used. In both cases, the input to the calculation is regulated by authorities. Here are some quotations from the article that illustrate this (p. 548):

> Operating expenses must be given in a disaggregated form and each part (e.g. Maintenance) balancing within a bandwidth set out in the guidance notes and in totalling at a minimum of 15% of the effective income.

> Capitalization rate within a bandwidth set out in the guidance note.

It is also mentioned that if a comparative method is used, a security discount of at least 10% should be made. The details of the calculation do not matter for the discussion here; the important characteristic is that the allowed inputs to the valuation are directly regulated by the authorities. This means that the authorities to a large extent determine the value that the banks should use when making lending decisions.

An historical example of a similar type of regulation can be found in one of the first public documents about property valuation in Sweden from 1752. The King regulated the minimum capitalization rates allowed when a property should be valued for lending purposes. The net revenue should be capitalized with a rate

---

3 RICS (2018, p. 3) states in a similar way that 'MLV is not an attempt to create a conservative market value or a market value under restrictive marketing conditions. It is a fully fledged alternative model with different underlying characteristics'.

that was not allowed to be below 6% for brick buildings and not below 7% for wood buildings (see Gustafsson et al. 2019).

RICS (2012, p. 70) also notes: 'These alternative bases may, and often do, involve prescribed approaches or assumptions and may therefore result in a value for the purpose of secured lending that is quite markedly different from market value'.

Bienert and Brunauer argue that international compatibility would be higher if MLV was defined as a derivative of market value. One factor leading to a reduction of the market value would be higher uncertainty. This uncertainty is then related to a risk analysis like the one described above, but also to the type of uncertainty discussed in Chapter 3, e.g. lack of comparable data (p. 556). In the article, they discuss in detail how such adjustments can be made.

Crosby and Hughes (2011) compared property values using market value, MLV and investment value. They used actual rents but would introduce 'some element of smoothing' if rents show a tendency to rise (p. 232). Capitalization rates are based on long-term historical data for the market in question and they argue that these 'introduce some form of objectivity to the valuation'. They, however, add 15% to the capitalization rate when calculating long-term values, in line with German recommendations for calculating MLV. Their interpretation of MLV is more of the type where MLV is derived from the market value through various adjustments – a strategy that will be discussed in the next section. A similar approach is developed and applied to Italian markets in Tajani and Morano (2018).

5.8 Alternative Value Concept (2) Worth or (Normalized) Investment Value

The definition in the International Valuation Standards (IVS) of Investment Value/Worth is the following (IVSC 2020 p. 22):

> Investment Value is the value of an asset to a particular owner or prospective owner for individual investment or operational objectives.
> Investment Value is an entity-specific basis of value. Although the value of an asset to the owner may be the same as the amount that could be realised from its sale to another party, this basis of value reflects the benefits received by an entity from holding the asset and, therefore, does not involve a presumed exchange. Investment Value reflects the circumstances and financial objectives of the entity for which the valuation is being produced.

Crosby et al. (2000) discuss another alternative to both market value and mortgage lending value, and that is a concept that they call 'worth' explained in the following way:

> ... market worth is the price at which an asset would trade on a market where sellers and buyers were using all available information in an efficient manner
>
> *(Crosby et al. 2000, p. 37).*

> With individual views on the inputs for an explicit cash flow analysis, it is possible to estimate individual worth: with consensus or market views, it is possible to estimate market worth
>
> *(Crosby et al. 2000, p. 38).*

As argued in Lind (2005), this concept has similar problems as mortgage lending value as it uses concepts that are difficult to observe and agree about. How do we know how buyers and sellers that are using all available information will act? How do they differ from the actual actors on the market? Does there really exist a market or consensus view in a market with many actors? Is it not more correct that on a market there always exist a diversity of views about how a certain area or property type will develop?

Crosby and Hughes (2011) use a concept that is similar to worth and that they call investment value (IV), but it is not based on a specific individual's views. They write:

> IV is an explicit cash flow model and the major inputs are market rent, rental growth rate, target rate of return (TR), holding period and exit capitalisation rate. (p. 231)

The inputs are taken from various official sources or from estimations by highly respected companies. Here are just two examples (p. 234):

> For rental value growth the model utilises the Investment Property Forum Consensus rental value growth forecasts of each sector for the five years ahead.

> cash flow is discounted at a TR based on the survey of target rates by DTZ within their money into property series
>
> *(DTZ, n.d.).*

> The exit value is a combination of the actual rental growth forecast on the rent capitalised at an exit capitalisation rate. This exit yield is based on the IPD equivalent yield series. Taking the average over the period 1981 (the date IPD first started measuring property performance in the UK) to the valuation date.

The idea is then to calculate the IV with data that are reflecting 'market views' and forecasts by leading actors on the market, and in that way a more objective IV can be calculated.

In their empirical study, they show that both mortgage lending value and IV, as they operationalize it, fluctuate less than the market value, and that these concepts therefore might give a more stable foundation for bank lending.

5.9 Derivatives of Market Value

In the interpretation of Crosby and Hughes (2011), mortgage lending value is more like a 'smoothed' market value. The idea that some kind of historical averages can be used as a more long-term value can also be found in Nordlund (2008). A concept called 'reference value' is introduced which is based on historical averages for all inputs in the valuation. The historical averages that are used depend on the valuation method chosen. If a direct comparative sales method is used, the historical average can be presented as value per sqm. If yields are used in the valuation, then the averages would be both both average net operating income over a period of time and average yields demanded.

A narrower interpretation of derivatives of market value is also possible and would mean that current and earlier market values are used without adjusting any inputs. A long-term value could, for example, be calculated as a moving average of earlier market values. Such a moving average could be used for lending decisions, but such an average can be higher than the current market value and it might be difficult to use such a value in a lending decision. A new concept – e.g. called 'Long-term lending value' – could be defined as the lowest of

a) current market value and
b) average market value during the last X years.

For properties where historical values are not available, a general index can be used to calculate the earlier values.

The idea is illustrated in Tables 5.1 and 5.2, where both the moving average is presented and the 'Long-term lending value' as defined above. In Table 5.1, a four-year moving average is used, and in Table 5.2, a six-year moving average.

If a four-year average is used, the 'long-term lending value' is 17% below the market value at the peak of the cycle. If a six-year average is used, the long-term lending value is 24% below the market value at the peak of the cycle. But Table 5.2 also illustrates a questionable feature of this kind of long-term value and that is that the long-term lending value goes up between year five and six even though the market value has fallen between these years. More complicated formulas can

Table 5.1 Illustration of using a moving average: four-year average.

Year	Market value	Four-year moving average	'Long-term lending value' (lowest of moving average and current value)
1	100		
2	110		
3	120		
4	140	117,5	117,5
5	160	132,5	132,5
6	130	137,5	130
7	110	135	110
8	100	125	100

Table 5.2 Illustration of using a moving average: six-year average.

Year	Market value	Six-year moving average	'Long-term lending value' (lowest of moving average and current value)
−1	110		
0	100		
1	100		
2	110		
3	120		
4	140	113	113
5	160	122	122
6	130	127	127
7	110	128	110
8	100	127	100

be used to avoid this – e.g. a rule saying that the long-term lending is not allowed to rise during a year that the market value falls.

If the bank uses a constant LTV-ratio in relation to a value like the long-term lending value as defined above, the effect is a lower LTV-ratio in relation to the market value during the boom, as would be rational if there is a belief in cycles. The result is therefore the same as using the ordinary market value but stipulating that the LTV-ratio should be reduced when there is a boom in the economy.

5.10   Cost-Based Value Concepts

Theoretical foundations for using some kind of cost-based value when thinking about the long-term value of a property can be found both in microeconomic theory and in simpler concepts like Tobin's q. The basic idea is that – as discussed briefly in Section 5.3 on price bubbles –if the price of a property is higher than the cost of production, then it should be expected that the more will be produced and that the increasing supply pushes the price down. Underestimation of future supply was one central factor behind price bubbles in the theory presented by Glaeser (2013). Keeping an eye on the cost of production would then be rational for a lending institution. Several cost concepts can be of interest in this context.

In accounting contexts, acquisition cost/-value has historically been very important when applying Historical Cost Accounting (HCA). The entry price at the time of acquisition for the acquirer is then the acquisition cost or cost of production. Today, many countries apply International Financial Reporting Standards (IFRS) and according to the standard IAS 40 (2020) – Investment Property, real estate assets falling within the definition of such properties, can be accounted for applying a fair value model or a cost model – see the next chapter. If applying the cost model in IAS 40, the owner of such properties will carry investment properties at historical cost in the balance sheet. The carrying amount will be reduced by depreciation for every reporting period. Fair value will be disclosed in notes to the accounts. Applying the fair value model, the companies holding such properties will carry properties at up-to-date fair value in the balance sheet in every reporting period.

Replacement cost is an entry price in accounting contexts and represents the amount that would be paid now to acquire the best asset available to undertake the function of the asset owned (less depreciation if appropriate).[4]

When using cost information as additional information in a lending decision, one must, however, also take into account that construction costs can change over the business cycle and that they typically fall during a recession.

5.11   Final Comment: Can Valuation Methods and Credit Rules Affect the Property Cycle?

Especially, after a down-turn in the economy and on the property market, there is a discussion if regulations for lending and value concepts would reduce the risk for cycles. Crosby and Hughes (2011, p. 238) ask 'Would the use of a different

---

4 See Kam (1990) and Penman (2007).

valuation regime have changed the nature of lending in the UK?'. Bienert and Brunauer (2007, p. 571) write:

> The mortgage lending valuation practice in German-speaking countries has proven in the past that the methods and concepts in principle are valuable and contribute to the stabilization of the whole financial system.

Anop-Engerstam (2015) investigates why house prices rose much less in Germany than in Sweden 2000–2015. Beside a well-functioning rental market, she points to a combination of valuation principles and lending practices as an explanation. In Germany, they used mortgage lending value instead of market value which meant that even if prices rose somewhat, it was not possible to borrow more. The banks demanded that the borrower should use long-term fixed interest rates, which during this period was higher than the short-term interest rates that most Swedish households chose. German banks also applied lower LTV-ratios and demanded quicker amortization. In Sweden, before the financial crises 2008–2009, it was possible to borrow 100% of the house price and there was no need to amortize. Anop-Engerstam finds that these differences in rules made it much more difficult for a potential buyer in Germany to borrow a larger amount and pay a higher price for a property.

Valuation for lending purposes also raises broader questions concerning the responsibility of the valuer to provide information that can contribute to a more rational market. We will return to this in Chapter 9 about governance and the role of the valuer.

One must not forget that in a world characterized by uncertainty, it is very difficult to find convincing evidence about future cash flows and/or future return requirements. This, of course, leads to problems when trying to estimate long-term values and we will return to these issues in the final chapter.

Exercises

1   Have there been discussions about bubbles in your local market: What are the main arguments presented for and against the existence of a bubble in the housing market or the commercial real estate market?

2   Interview local banks about how they do risk analysis when lending to commercial property.

3 Interview local banks and regulators about value concepts used when lending to commercial property.

4 Pro and con: Is some kind of long-term value motivated or is it enough to use the concept of market value?

6

Valuation for Financial Reports and Other Accounting-Related Issues

6.1 Introduction

In the balance sheet of a company, the assets of the company must be reported. Today, the same holds for many public authorities. Real estate is an important asset in many companies, and this raises the issue how assets should be valued for balance sheet purposes.

Earlier, the starting point for the values in a balance sheet was what the owner historically had paid for the property, so-called Historical Cost Accounting (HCA). This could be a construction cost or a purchasing price. This initial amount should then be depreciated with some percent every year over the estimated useful life of the asset. If the properties were improved, the value in the balance sheet could be increased, but typically the rules for this were rather restrictive. Instead of being capitalized as an asset in the balance sheet, the expenses were often classified as a maintenance cost that immediately was deducted from the revenue of the company in the income statement. The outlays affected the yearly result, and as part of that, the net operating income in the income statement, but not the value of the asset in the balance sheet.

One restriction was typically that the value of the property in the balance sheet was not allowed to be higher than the current market value. An exception could be if the lower value were judged to be temporary.

These old rules had the consequence that the balance sheet, on many occasions, did not really say much about the economic situation of the company. Maybe the real value of the assets was much higher than the value in the accounts, because of investments made or because of rising prices in the market. Especially during periods of high inflation, the nominal values in the accounts soon lost their relevance.

These problems led to a radical change in the accounting rules, at least for companies above a certain size. The new rules - IFRS fair value model in IAS 40 - say

Advanced Issues in Property Valuation, First Edition. Hans Lind and Bo Nordlund.
© 2021 John Wiley & Sons Ltd. Published 2021 by John Wiley & Sons Ltd.

that the value in the accounts should reflect the 'fair value' of the property and that changes in fair value should be reported in the income statement as valuation-gains or -losses.

In this chapter, a number of issues related to valuation and accounting will be discussed. Section 6.2 discusses the fair value concept and the interpretation of exit price, Section 6.3 looks at the 'fair value hierarchy' and disclosure requirements. Section 6.4 covers the issue of valuation of public sector building and in Section 6.5 we discuss some issues related to depreciation and free cash flows from property investments. In Section 6.6, there is a short discussion about a topic closely related to financial reporting – auditing of fair values. This can be described as a kind of quality assurance of figures and other information reported in financial reports. Finally, there are some concluding comments on accounting rules in Section 6.7.

6.2   The Fair Value Concept

In the accounting literature, the concept of fair value is central. IFRS 13 (2020), produced by International Accounting Standards Board (IASB), defines the Fair Value for the purposes of financial reporting. The definition and further description of the fair-value concept can be found below with references to relevant paragraphs in the standard.

> This IFRS defines fair value as the price that would be received to sell an asset or paid to transfer a liability in an orderly transaction between market participants at the measurement date. (para 9)

This is expanded in the following way, where it is clarified that fair value refers to an exit price.

> Fair value is the price that would be received to sell an asset or paid to transfer a liability in an orderly transaction in the principal (or most advantageous) market at the measurement date under current market conditions (ie an exit price) regardless of whether that price is directly observable or estimated using another valuation technique. (para 24)

In the appendix 'Defined terms', an appendix that is an integral part of the IFRS, it is also clarified that the actors should be knowledgeable and not be forced or otherwise compelled. This clearly shows the similarity between the market value definition and the fair value definition. It is also clarified that the actors must be able to enter into a transaction of the asset at the fair value; otherwise the definition is not fulfilled.

Our conclusion is that there is no fundamental difference between Market value and Fair value as described in IFRS 13. RICS (2019) expresses the same standpoint on this issue. Value assessment in accordance with the definition of market value should in all essential aspects work as estimation of fair value according to IFRS 13, and the other way around. A detailed comparison between the concept of market value and (an earlier definition of) fair value can be found in Deaconu and Buiga (2010), where they conclude that differences more concern the extent to which the documents offer technical details and disclosure requirements (p. 379).

Usually a valuation is made at a certain point in time (the value date) and used for a lending decision or in a transaction. When the lending or the transaction is carried out, it is not so important if the value stays the same or not. It is not important to value the object again after a short period of time. An exception to this is valuation for financial reporting purposes since IFRS requires the updated fair value to be estimated and reported for every reporting period. When the fair value concept is defined, it is underlined that it is an exit price. This raises the question if we can assume that if a buyer has paid the price P, the property has an exit price of P after the transaction has been carried out (see Lind and Nordlund 2019 for a more detailed discussion of this and the case below).

On a market with a large number of similar properties and many well-informed actors, it should be expected that the demand curve is almost horizontal (for a transaction volume within a certain interval) at the price that is rational to pay. The actors on the market know the market value of the property and no one is willing to pay more than this expected market value. When new information arrives, the demand curve shifts, but still all (active) participants on the market would be willing to pay about the same amount. French and Gabrielli (2018) put it 'If the market is efficient it is likely that this price will reflect the consensus view' (p. 394).

In such markets, the concept of market value, and accounting rules linked to market value or exit price, seem rather unproblematic. If someone buys a property at the market value P, it would be no problem for that actor to sell the property for approximately P the next day, unless new information has arrived during the day. Entry price and exit price would be the same.

Most markets for commercial properties are, however, rather thin with a relatively small number of actors, and where the actors, on many occasions, can be expected to have different reservation prices for the property. The difference in reservation prices can both be related to expected net income and to different views about the risk and the rational rate of return that should be demanded. An example can illustrate a typical situation.

Let us assume that company S is planning to sell a large commercial property. The company believes that there are four potential buyers and estimates that these companies have the reservation prices listed in Table 6.1.

Table 6.1 Assumed reservation prices.

Company	Reservation price as estimated by the seller
A	1200
B	1000
C	900
D	800

Let us furthermore assume that these estimated reservation prices are approximately correct. A case where this is not true will be commented on below. If the seller auctioned the property with a standard English auction, or with a second-price auction, the price would be 1000+ε given the reservation prices in Table 6.1.

The first thing we can note, in line with the discussion about auctions in Klemperer (2004), is that in a thin market a rational and well-informed seller would not use a standard English auction, or a second-price auction. If the selling company believes that company A is willing to pay 1200, the seller would not be satisfied with a price of 1000. If the reservation prices in practice are common knowledge, and if the buyer and seller bargain in line with standard game theory, they would split the 200 of added value if the property is sold to A in half. The most probable price - the market value - would then be 1100.

Assume now that company A, after buying the property for 1100, shall estimate the value of the property for balance sheet purposes. If the property were auctioned off with an English auction, the price would be 900+ε. If the seller used the information/estimation of the reservation prices in the way company S did, then company A would get a price of 950.

It might, however, be the case that when companies B, C and D observe that company A paid 1100 for the property, the other companies see this as new information indicating that maybe they underestimated the value. If these other companies all increased their reservation prices by 50, then the auction would yield a price of 950 and a bargaining procedure might lead to a price of 1000, as the reservation price of company B would now be 1050.

The conclusion so far is that in a rational thin market where the transaction as such does not give (much) new information, *the exit price immediately after the transaction should be lower than the price that the current owner paid*. The most probable price is lower when the actor that had the highest reservation price is no longer on the market. *The value for accounting purposes should then be set below the price that the company paid for the property*.

Benston (2008) discusses another problem with using exit prices and that is the risk for manipulations, e.g. possible management bias when making estimations of fair value as discussed by Selling and Nordlund (2015). In the above case, company A may, after it has bought the property for 1100 (with a reservation price of 1200), argue that there 'now' are several other companies who have understood that the property has a high value. These other companies now also have a reservation price of 1200. If there are two such companies, the exit price would be 1200-ε. Company A could therefore argue that the value of the property in the accounts should be increased to 1200. The company can then report a profit of 100.

The general conclusion from this section is that current rules, focusing on exit price, imply that downgrades of property values in balance sheets should be rather common in a stable market. Our experience is, however, that such downgrades are rare. The arguments in this section suggest that stricter rules might be needed to make it difficult to at least increase the reported value close to initial recognition of an acquired property – if the owner recently won a bidding contest and if no new essential information is present.

6.3 The Fair Value Hierarchy, Disclosure Requirements and the Risk for Bias

An interesting aspect of the regulation around valuation and accounting is that the regulator explicitly through the fair value hierarchy has pointed out what kind of data is most reliable. As mentioned in Chapter 3, the hierarchy concerns inputs in valuation models. These inputs are divided into different levels related to the quality of the input. The IFRS 13 gives no preference for certain methods over others, but it clarifies that the inputs can be divided into observable and unobservable inputs; and that a company as far as possible should use relevant observable inputs in the valuation. The company should minimize the use of inputs that are more difficult to observe. The hierarchy is summarized below (see also Chapter 3):

Level 1 = Inputs require no adjustments, based on quoted prices (for example, if the valuation object is a share in a listed company, it can be monitored on the stock exchange. It can be observed what exactly the same instrument is worth on the market).

Level 2 = Inputs which are directly or indirectly observable from the market and require different degrees of adjustments (e.g. comparable properties sold in the property market, close in time in relation to the value date and sold objects whose other characteristics[1] are not significantly different from the valuation object). Level 2 inputs require less significant adjustments to be relevant.

---

1 For instance - site/location, type of property, rental income level, vacancy level, or technical condition.

Level 3 = Unobservable inputs. This group may also include input from the market that requires significant adjustments. Examples of the latter might be comparable objects sold on the property market which occurred further back in time or when the sold objects' other characteristics differ significantly from the valuation object. Level 3 inputs are usually determined based on management's assumptions.

In a European Real Estate IFRS 13-survey performed by PWC (2014), 97% of the reviewed companies identified inputs in the valuation of investment properties as falling within Level 3 of the fair value hierarchy. Nordlund et al. (2020, 2021) also conclude that investment properties are usually valued by applying Level 3 inputs in valuation models. The reliability of fair values is discussed in Nellessen and Zuelch (2011) and reliability is linked to the level of the inputs.

Earlier versions of IAS 40 required companies to disclose the applied methods and significant assumptions made in the valuation of investment properties. The standard, IAS 40, also stated at that point in time that the disclosure of applied methods and significant assumptions should include a statement whether the determination of fair value was supported by market evidence or was more heavily based on other factors (which the entity had to disclose) because of the nature of the property and lack of comparable market data. Nordlund (2010) concluded that disclosure regarding applied methods, significant assumptions in property valuations and statements about the connections between appraised values and market evidence needed refinement in financial reports. As the uncertainty in property valuations cannot be removed, it has to be managed. Providing explicit disclosure about valuations is one important way to manage this issue by reducing the gap of information asymmetry between those who perform valuations, or prepare financial reports, and those who are users of financial statements. Today, most of the required disclosures about inputs in valuations can be found in IFRS 13 instead of in IAS 40, and are in part formulated differently than they were in IAS 40. The intention is still that users of financial statements shall get the information they need to make good investment decisions when allocating capital to investments, e.g. investment in properties.

In this context, it is also of great importance to be aware of the nature of information asymmetry, according to the agency theory. This situation could occur when, for instance, the management and other preparers of financial statements know more about the qualities of the valuation of properties held by the company than the users of the financial reports. The usefulness of financial reports for investors and the reports' contribution to an efficient market depends on the quality and amount of information that is disclosed.

There are several studies that present evidence that management bias can occur in this situation (see, e.g. Selling and Nordlund 2015; Oyewo et al. 2020), especially as it is difficult for auditors to question the value reported by professional valuers (see e.g. Joe et al. 2017; Ahn et al. 2019). Baum et al. (2000) show that fund managers try to reduce the value of the properties when the manager is new, as a lower initial variation can lead to better results and higher bonuses. Mäki (2020) finds evidence that firms that use valuers from smaller firms show higher increases in the value of the properties.

6.4 Valuation of Public Sector Properties

Public sector properties can be valued in a number of different contexts (see Lind and Lundström 1996 for an early overview). If a property should be sold on the open market, an ordinary market value is sought and standard valuation methods should be used. Accounting rules in the public sector have become more similar to the ones in the private sector. In order to make decisions more professional, Infrastructure asset management systems have been introduced and in these systems, valuations of assets are also important, see, e.g. IAM (2015).

There are a number of problems with the choice of value concepts in this context. Public sector assets have been privatized in some countries and this means that there exists a market for such properties. Let us take an electricity grid as an example. How much a private actor is willing to pay for such a grid will to a large extent depend on the rules imposed, especially rules about the price that the private actor is allowed to charge for such a natural monopoly. If the firm is allowed to charge a high price, or believe they will be able to charge a high price, then the investor is willing to pay a high price. The same kind of situation arises in a sale-leaseback transaction, e.g. when a local authority wants to sell a school and at the same time lease it back with perhaps a 20-year contract. The price that the private actor is willing to pay will here to a large extent depend on what rent the local authority is willing to pay. One can, for example, imagine a situation where the local authority needs money and, for some reason, do not want to borrow, and then they may be willing to sign a contract with a high rent in order to get a high price when they enter into the sale-leaseback transaction. Hordijk et al. (2010), for example, show that rents in sale-leaseback transactions on average were above market rents.

For properties owned by the public sector, it is common to recommend some kind of cost-based value, either because transactions do not occur or that the prices are endogenous, as argued in the paragraph above. Cost-based valuations can be relevant for systems where privatization is not on the agenda, e.g. the water and sewage system in a city. As described in basic textbooks, a typical cost-based valuation method starts with calculating the replacement cost and then depreciates this for wear and tear and for functional obsolescence. Such a value does, however, have some rather counterintuitive properties.

If efficiency in the construction sector improves, then replacement cost and value will fall. The asset value can therefore fall both because something 'good' happens (lower construction cost) and because something 'bad' happens (e.g. increased obsolescence). One has to think carefully about what the point is of determining an asset value and what methods are relevant. A reasonable starting point is the user of the information presented in a public sector balance sheet and what different users should be interested in. Over the years, we have seen misuse of property valuations in this context, e.g. when a health provider that was criticized for not having put aside enough funds for future pensions responded by making a revaluation of the hospital buildings. The new values were considerably higher, and the authority then argued that it had enough assets. But it is hardly a realistic or sustainable option to sell the core buildings to get cash to pay pensions with! Especially, if a sale-leaseback contract includes a high rent payment.

6.5 Property Depreciation, Refurbishments and Free Cash Flows to the Property Firm

According to IAS 40 (2020) — Investment Property, a company shall disclose separately the additions of investment property assets attributable to acquisitions of investment property (A), subsequent expenditures attributable to existing investment properties (B) and finally, additions resulting from acquisitions through business combinations (C). The question is how to decide what costs should be included in each category above — A, B or C? Acquisitions of investment property (A) should include asset acquisitions/wrappers, newly erected buildings and significant extensions of buildings leading to larger rentable area. Subsequent expenditure (B) consists largely of the replacement of components or creating new components, redevelopment, refurbishments attributable to existing properties/buildings. Acquisitions attributable to business combinations (C) are those falling within the scope of IFRS 3 – Business Combinations (See IFRS 3 2020).

IFRS-standards are based on the way in which different actors use financial reports in making economic decisions on the basis of financial statements. The need to keep properties up-to-date in a market, where properties are exposed to competition, normally results in large cash outflows (subsequent expenditure, type B above) which are not reflected in the Income Statement. Income Statement figures only show the net rental/net operating income, where maintenance cost like day-to-day servicing and replacement of minor parts is expensed in the income statement. The fact that not all subsequent expenditure, needed to keep the properties up-to-date, can be found in income statement figures alone could lead to overestimation of the free cash-flows from property companies if the analysts fail to get adequate information from the notes to the financial statements (disclosures). Our view is that more emphasis should be placed on how property companies interpret and categorize capitalized costs (so-called capex) according to IAS 40 and the classification (A, B and C) described earlier.

Studies of listed property companies in Sweden suggest that there are different interpretations in this respect. This can lead to frustration among analysts in trying to analyse the free cash-flows from the property companies. The vast majority (90–95%) of listed property companies in Europe apply the fair value model in IAS 40 and show no depreciation charge in the Income Statement. However, showing no depreciation in the income statement does not mean that there is no consumption of the benefits associated with property assets or parts of such assets. Instead of a depreciation charge in the Income Statement, such consumption can be seen by analysing the levels of maintenance expenditures and capex that are in fact cash outflows to keep properties up-to-date and competitive in the market (type B above). To determine the free cash-flows produced by a property company, one must deduct this 'maintenance capex' from the net rental/net operating income showed in the income statement. Of course, central administration costs should also be deducted when calculating the free cash-flow to the firm (FCFF).

In conclusion, property companies need to use similar classifications when dividing cost into A, B and C as discussed above, and probably there is also a need for separate disclosure of the FCFF in line with the definition above.

6.6 Auditing and Quality Assurance of Fair Values in Financial Reporting

Closely connected to accounting and financial reporting is also the issue of auditing. Auditing can, among other things, be described as a process of quality assurance of information in the financial reports. This, in turn, is important for markets to work well and be efficient. Investment properties presented according to IFRS (IAS 40 (2020) – Investment Property) can be appraised by independent valuers (recommended)[2] or by internal valuers. Selling and Nordlund (2015) discuss the risk of management bias and state that the standards of the PCAOB[3] implicitly, yet unmistakably, presume that auditors are capable of eliminating the effects of management bias. In this context, it can be interesting to note that significant concerns have been raised about audit quality regarding accounting estimates and that there is a need to address this by fostering a more independent

---

2 See IAS 40 para 32.
3 Public Company Accounting Oversight Board.

and challenging sceptical mindset in auditors (see, for instance, Selling and Nordlund 2015; Joe et al. 2017; Ahn et al. 2019; IAASB 2019).

Joe et al. (2017) discuss that outside observers have brought to attention that auditors on many occasions rely too heavily on evidence from client specialists, and do not adjust the audit approach based on the level of client risk. They also note that the implications of their findings are troublesome for investors because their theory predicts that the degree of quantification in client-provided evidence reduces the likelihood that auditors will apply subjective procedures (including developing independent estimates) to test FV inputs that are most prone to management bias and opportunism. Selling and Nordlund (2015) discuss the risk of management bias in real estate fair value-estimates and argue that it should be preferable to have objective external valuation expertise providing the valuations which then are presented in financial reports. There should be strong restrictions on the management's ability to influence the values. Furthermore, they argue that there could be a need for fundamental changes to the rules of engagement between the auditor and the client. Their idea is to incrementally over time, transfer the responsibility for financial statement judgements to independent appraisers. Auditing would then become solely a verification service, and financial statements would better serve investors and the public interest. Oyewo et al. (2020) describe the risk of management manipulating earnings owing to the inability of auditors to effectively test fair value estimates and the difficulty in testing unobservable inputs in valuation models.

Nordlund et al. (2020, 2021) remark that the transparency in the property market is lacking and that there is a risk that auditors may end up with confirmation bias and anchoring (see also what was discussed about these issues in Chapter 4). They also underline that fair values of investment properties are normally estimated applying Level 3 inputs. The results from their study indicate that there might be a lack of understanding, and sometimes questionable interpretations, of the relevant value concept among auditors - fair value according to IFRS 13. The authors also take up the issue of different value concepts and conclude that there are strong indications that the auditors, on many occasions, cannot be sufficiently sure whether the values presented in the balance sheets are closer to investment values (from the current owners' point of view) or, as it should be, fair values in accordance with the definition in IFRS 13. They also raise some concerns regarding the auditors' perception of the most suitable valuation method(s)/approach(es) and the need for market information when estimating fair values, especially in so-called thin markets.

A suggestion that emerged from the study by Nordlund et al. (2020, 2021) is that auditors may need to hire/employ independent valuers on their behalf, performing some valuations of investment properties in audit engagements before they review the valuations presented by management to avoid risk of anchoring and confirmation bias. They suggest that preferably these experts should be hired by auditors and would be other valuers than those used by the company preparing their financial reports. If there are material differences between the estimates by the independent expert hired by the auditor and the estimation presented by the company/management, such differences should be given extra attention and discussed/analysed before deciding how to act on such information, see also what was discussed earlier in this book, regarding valuation methods, about so-called actor-based approaches when estimating fair (market) values.

6.7 Concluding Comments About Fair Values

The arguments for having fair values (market values) in the accounts are clear as information about market values give more information about the true standing of the company in the current situation than stale historical cost-based figures. The regulators, however, seem to have underestimated the problems that can occur when market values play an important role in the accounts. Market values can be difficult to estimate and as discussed in earlier chapters, there are ways for the companies to influence the reported values. There are legal ways to do that as discussed earlier, e.g. by not selling when prices would be below a certain level. Market values can be kept up by reducing supply if valuations are based on information from transaction-markets and not taking into account other kinds of market information as discussed above in the context of actor-based approaches.

It is interesting to think about how the regulations might be changed without returning to the old system. Applications of IFRS in European companies are now around 15 years old and our opinion is that it is time for a serious evaluation of whether the system has accomplished the goals that were set up. Our experience, in line with the arguments in Benston (2008), is that the room for manipulation is too large today, and that it could be questioned whether the rules concerning exit price are followed in practice.

Maybe some combination of the old and the new rules could be better, e.g. that revaluations only can be made with larger intervals and/or that changes in values in the balance sheet should follow some kind of moving average model. It is emphasized in the accounting standard that clear empirical evidence is crucial when a company wants to report valuation gains, but it should be interesting to evaluate how this is interpreted in practice in different countries. Another way forward could be that IASB prescribes that only assets valued with Level 1 inputs should be allowed to be carried at fair value on a continuing basis in the balance sheet (with possible effects in the income statement). Assets valued with Level 3 inputs should not be allowed to be continually revalued to fair value in the balance sheet. It can be argued that assets valued with Level 3 inputs instead could be presented as information in the notes to the accounts on assessed fair value, which will be the case when applying the cost model in IAS 40 (2020) – Investment Property. In our view, asset values estimated from Level 3 inputs are not suitable to be carried on a continuing basis at fair value in the balance sheet, at least not for real estate assets in thin markets. This would also mean that such changes should not be reported in the income statement.

Exercises

1 Interview real estate companies in your local market about how they estimate fair values, how they classify various expenses and how auditors evaluate fair values in financial reports.

2 Let us go back to the question in Chapter 3 about market value estimation in a situation like the one below.

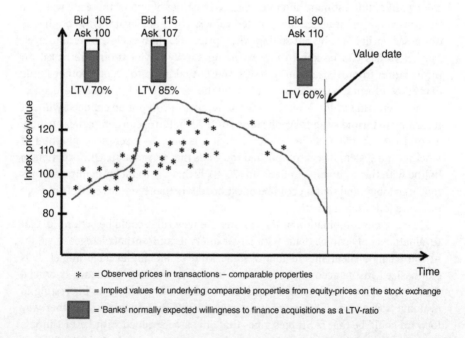

*   = Observed prices in transactions – comparable properties

—— = Implied values for underlying comparable properties from equity-prices on the stock exchange

▇   = 'Banks' normally expected willingness to finance acquisitions as a LTV-ratio

We now move into the accounting and auditing issues. Recall your reasoning regarding what fair/market value is, given this information from the market. Next, you look at the accounting information in a property company holding similar properties. The fair value according to earlier financial reports from this company is illustrated below:

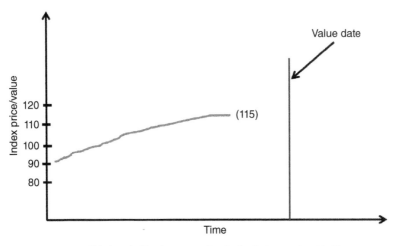

= Fair (market) value according to the balance sheet in the company

Based on the discussions you had when solving the exercise in Chapter 3, what fair/market value figure would you suggest the company (expressed as an index-level, e.g. 120, 100, 80) to report at the value date? What effects would that give in the balance sheet (carrying amount of investment property) and in the income statement?

3   Pro and con: Combine your reasoning in the last question with what you have learned earlier about lack of transparency in the property markets, client influence/-pressure on valuers, uncertainty in property valuations and discuss these issues from different point of views (the valuer, the management in the company, the auditor). Take the standpoint of either the valuer, the management in the company and an independent auditor. How would you as a representative of either of these groups argue about the reasonableness of a certain value? Is it possible to agree on a value figure that all three parties find acceptable? Why, why not?

4   Pro and con: Are the current fair value rules the best or is there a need to make changes in the regulations in order to avoid management bias? The latter group should present an alternative to the current system.

7

Property Valuation and Sustainable Buildings

7.1 Introduction

Issues related to sustainability and climate change affect all areas in society and property valuation is no exception. RICS (2019, p. 72) notes that 'Sustainability factors are becoming a more significant market influence'.[1] On the most general level, it can affect the role of professionals, including valuers, and raise issues about the responsibility of a professional and the role of private companies. These issues will be discussed in Chapter 9 on governance and ethics.

In this chapter, the perspective is narrower, and the focus is on valuation issues related to the individual building and aspects that can arise when a green/sustainable building is to be valued. In Section 7.2, the concept of green/sustainable building is discussed more in detail, including environmental certification schemes. Why green buildings might have a higher value is discussed in Section 7.3 – the existence of a green premium. Section 7.4 discusses valuation methods from the perspective of sustainability and green buildings. A more special issue is covered in Section 7.5 and that is, that for a 'brown' building, there is an option to make it green and this might reduce the difference in value between brown and green buildings. Final comments can be found in Section 7.6.

7.2 What Is a Green/Sustainable Building – on Environmental Certification Systems

There are a number of environmental certification systems. The internationally most well-known are BREEAM and LEED, but many countries also have national systems that are widely used, e.g. Energy Star in the United States. Each system

---

1 An overview of research on issues related to real estate and sustainability can be found in *The Routledge Handbook of Sustainable Real Estate*, 2018.

Advanced Issues in Property Valuation, First Edition. Hans Lind and Bo Nordlund.
© 2021 John Wiley & Sons Ltd. Published 2021 by John Wiley & Sons Ltd.

might also have a number of specific versions targeted on specific types of buildings or on stages in the life cycle of the building. There are also certification schemes for larger areas. In the boxes below, there is a short presentation of LEED and BREEM. An overview of systems can be found in Braun and Bienert (2015).

LEED (www.usgbc.org/about/brand)
The US Green Building Council is responsible for LEED. The first version was launched in 1998 and today there are a number of different versions. There are, for example, versions for existing building and for new construction. There are also versions for whole cities and communities. The history of the system is described on the web-address above.

The system is based on point-system covering a large number of aspects and based on the number of points, buildings can be classified as Platinum, Gold, Silver and Certified.

BREEAM https://www.breeam.com
BREEAM (Building Research Establishment Environmental Assessment Method) is an initially British system that was launched in the early 1990s. It has also developed into a global diversified certification system with models for new building, existing buildings and masterplanning projects. BREEAM has the same basic structure as LEED with points set on a number of aspects leading up to a total score that determines the final classification in Outstanding, Excellent, Very Good, Good, Pass and Unclassified.

From a property valuation perspective, it is important to be aware of the following:

1) Some certification systems focus only on the characteristics of the building as such, which means that the location of the building does not affect the label. Others are broader and take into account locational aspects, e.g. the possibility to access the building with environmentally friendly transport systems. As location is important for property values, it should be expected that the second type of label influences the property value more.
2) Broader systems like LEED and BREEAM may differ in exactly which dimensions that are included. As the dimensions can be expected to differ in importance for potential buyers or tenants, it is very important to know what is covered and what is not covered in a specific system.
3) Almost all systems consider several different aspects. An exception was the system EU-green building that only took energy use into account. When there

are several different dimensions, these must be aggregated in some way and this may also differ between systems. If there is a point system where points for qualities in different dimensions are added up, it is important to know what dimensions give most points. A strategic builder will evaluate how costly it is to get high points in different dimensions and focus on 'cheap' points, and accept lower points in dimensions where it is costly to get a high point. These dimensions might, however, not be the dimensions that are most important from a property valuation perspective.

4) As noted in DeLisle et al. (2013), the certification systems have changed over time and this also creates problems from a valuation perspective. An older and a newer building that has the same environmental certificate may not have the same qualities as the certification system may have changed somewhat over time. The change can affect both dimensions included and how they are valued in the system.

5) A final problem concerns demands for measurement and follow-ups in the system. This also differs between systems which can make it hard to know if the current characteristics of the building are the same as when the building was certified. A number of studies have, for example, shown that actual energy use in low-energy buildings can be considerably higher than expected from the often theoretical calculations that the initial certification is based on.

One lesson from this is that, it is important to have information about the actual current characteristics of the building in order to evaluate how sustainable it really is, e.g. real-time measurements of energy use. Since some of the aspects of sustainable buildings are expected to affect productivity – see the next section – measures of customer satisfaction are also important. As discussed in the final section, new data collection methods and 'big data' may make it easier to follow the characteristics of a building over time.

There are also classification systems that focus on the company instead of the individual properties. An example is the system MSCI-ESG which evaluates real estate companies from the perspectives of environment, social and governance aspects (see https://www.msci.com/esg-ratings).

7.3 How Sustainability Can Affect Property Values

7.3.1 From an Investment Value Perspective

On a rational market, individual investment values will determine property prices and values. One way to approach the question how sustainability affects property values is then to look at the components in an investment value calculation. This is done in a very systematic way in Lorenz and Lützkendorf (2008, 2011) and the following factors may lead to a higher value on a sustainable commercial building. Here, we look only at the characteristics of the building as such.

- *Higher rents*: If, for example, the sustainable building has a better indoor climate, then tenants would be willing to pay more. There might also be signalling effects where tenants want to signal their environmental awareness by renting space in a sustainable building. If the tenant pays the heating cost, then lower heating costs should lead to higher relative rents.
- *Lower vacancy*: At a given rent level, it should be expected that tenants would prefer an office in a green building even if productivity is the same as there still would be a signalling effect.
- *Lower operating costs*: The main argument for lower operating costs is of course lower energy-use.
- Higher rents, lower vacancy and lower operating costs lead to higher *net operating income*.
- *Rate of return demanded*: The argument for using a lower rate of return on a sustainable building is that some risks would be lower. If energy prices go up, a sustainable building would be affected less. If there are new regulations to counteract the use of fossil fuels, then buildings that already are more sustainable would be affected less (see, e.g. French and Antill 2018). If a building is certified, it means that an independent agency has evaluated the building and this should in itself reduce the general risk, e.g. the risk that there are hidden problems in the building. There are, however, also arguments in the other direction. Sustainable buildings typically use newer and more advanced technical solutions, and the technical risks may therefore be higher in the sustainable buildings. If there are beliefs that the rent would increase more in sustainable buildings and/or that they will depreciate slower, then that would be an argument for using a lower initial yield when valuing the building. A discussion of sustainability and risk can be found in Meins and Sager (2015).

It should be noted that even if each of these differences is rather small, the total effect can be rather large. The example presented in Table 7.1 illustrates this.

Table 7.1 The effect of sustainability on value: an hypothetical example.

	Ordinary building	Green building
Rent	100	103
Operating cost	30	28
Net operating income	70	75
Initial yield demanded	0.07	0.063
Property value	1000	1190

In this case, the sustainable building would be worth almost 20% more than the ordinary building even though the difference for each individual factor is rather small.

7.3.2 From a Portfolio Perspective and Brand Perspective

As the importance of sustainability grows in most societies, it can be interesting to invest in sustainable buildings even if the direct economic gains from the sustainable buildings are not higher than in other buildings. Especially, pension funds and insurance companies can have CSR-policies that include environmental goals. This can make investment in sustainable buildings as one part of their portfolio more interesting (see, e.g. Brooks and McArthur 2019). Geiger et al. (2016) find that owning shares in green real estate companies can add to the value of an investor's portfolio. From a company perspective, investing in sustainable buildings can also open up new sources of finance, e.g. green bonds.

From a valuation perspective, these factors can be described in terms of investors reducing the direct rate of return that they demand from the investment as the property adds other value than the direct pay-off. This requirement for lower rate of return in turn increases the price that some investors are willing to pay and can lead to higher market values.

7.3.3 From a Climate Change Perspective

So far in this chapter, sustainable buildings have primarily been discussed from the perspective of the environmentally friendliness of the building. But climate change can affect the value of all buildings, especially in the long run. As mentioned in the last chapter, this is important for banks that lend money to real estate as climate change can affect the value of their collateral in the long run. All long-term investors have, however, reason to carefully analyse how climate change can affect the relative value of different properties.

A number of studies have investigated how far current prices already take these factors into account. The most obvious factors to investigate are the risk for flooding as a consequence of rising sea levels or risks related to extreme weather (damage from flooding, fire and storms). Example of studies are Bélanger et al. (2018), Hirsch and Hahn (2018) and Miller et al. (2019).

Policy reactions like to climate change, like higher fossil fuel taxes, can, for example, affect the relative cost of transport and thereby the relative attractiveness of different locations.

The value of the building will, however, also depend on the possibility to insure the building and the availability of state guarantees. Economists have, for example, pointed out that subsidized insurances can lead to wrong locational choices that increase the damages from extreme weather.

7.4 Valuation Methods and Sustainable Buildings

From the perspective of determining the market value of a property, different degrees of sustainability is just another dimension in which properties might differ. There is therefore no need to think in terms of special valuation methods.

Initially, the number of green building on a market was very low and then it was difficult to find comparable objects in the market. It was then important to make the correct judgement about how much more the investors on the specific market would be willing to pay for the green building. All the different adjustment methods discussed in Chapter 3 are relevant in this situation. Runde and Thoyre (2010) discussed this in terms of sustainability take-up in the local market.

An adjustment using a cash-flow analysis could start from differences in rent levels and operating costs that leads to different net operating incomes. Differences in rate of return demanded can lead to further adjustment and to differences in the net present values between green and non-green buildings. From this, the effect on the market value could be evaluated. A more actor-based approach would be based on knowledge of how different actors are reasoning and if there are funds that want to have a certain share of green buildings. Looking at value differences between green and non-green buildings on other markets can also give guidance about this difference in the current market.

There are today a large number of scientific papers published on the relation between the greenness of a building and the prices observed on the market. Some recent examples are Robinson and McAllister (2015) and Oyedokun et al. (2018), where further references can be found.

7.5 The Relation Between Values of 'Green' and 'Brown' Buildings

7.5.1 Short-Run and Long-Run

There have been academic discussions about 'green premiums' (or 'brown discounts') and how they may develop over time. What will happen when the number of green buildings increases? Standard microeconomic theory is a suitable tool to analyse questions like this. Microeconomic theory makes a clear distinction between short-run and long-run. Let us start with the short-run, which in this context can be seen as a 5–10 year period. If green buildings produce higher value, either through higher productivity for users or through lower operating cost, then differences in value will remain even if the number of green buildings increases. These underlying factors make the individual investment value higher even if supply increases.

If price differences today to a large extent depend on other factors, e.g. CSR goals and company image, then it should be expected that increasing the number of green buildings will reduce the green premium. Initially, a number of investors with CSR-goal will compete over a small number of green buildings and this will drive up the price. If more and more green buildings are available on the market, this image effect would fall and the price difference between green and non-green buildings would fall to the level that is motivated by the underlying fundamental factors (productivity, operating cost). It is, of course, possible to imagine that image-related demand for sustainable buildings increases at the same time as supply, and then the brand-related green premium would remain.

Several studies have looked at the location of green buildings within a city (e.g. Braun and Bienert 2015). The typical result is that green buildings initially were built in central locations, and this indicates that it was a small group of high-status firms that were willing to pay extra for sustainability. Later, green buildings were constructed also in less central locations and a possible explanation is that more firms were willing to pay for increased sustainability. Another possible explanation is that the cost of construction for green buildings fell and that therefore these buildings would be interesting also for companies whose willingness to pay for the green qualities were a little lower.

In the long run, the relative cost of producing buildings with different levels of sustainability will be important. Some studies (e.g. Zalejska-Jonsson et al. 2012) indicate that the cost of production for green buildings is only marginally higher than for non-green buildings. If the green buildings have higher value because of higher productivity and lower operating costs, then we should expect that only green buildings will be produced. This is something we can observe in some markets, e.g. in the office market in Sweden where practically all new office buildings are environmentally certified to a relatively high level. The 'brown' buildings will then step by step be phased out through demolition or through renovation that leads to more sustainable buildings. A process that can be quicker if there are tax advantages to green buildings.

Sustainability is not an either/or category and there are different grades in the systems described above. The same type of argument as above is also relevant when demand for different degrees of sustainability is studied. Some firms will be willing to pay for the highest degree of sustainability for any of the reasons described above. Other may be satisfied with a somewhat lower level.

7.5.2 From a Real-Option Perspective

In the section 'Highest and Best Use' in Chapter 2, it was noted that a property typically includes a number of 'real options'. There are possibilities to change the property in different ways, even though there may be disagreement and different levels of knowledge about these options among actors on the market. In the chapter about valuation methods, there was a short section on valuing real options.

There are a number of aspects related to sustainable buildings that can be looked at from an option perspective. As discussed in Vimpari and Junnila (2014), systems of environmental certification can be seen as giving a new 'option' to real estate owners. Should the owner certify the building or not? Should the property owner wait and certify in the future instead of certifying now?

From a valuation perspective, this option perspective could be most important when appraising 'brown' buildings. Let us assume that green certified buildings have a higher value, either because of direct economic benefits or from the portfolio effect. Brown buildings can differ in how costly it is to transform them into a building that can get a green certification. In a rational market, a brown building that is not costly to make green should have a higher value than others, because in this case the option to make it green would have a high value. In a real estate market one can find investors who are looking for 'mispriced' properties, i.e. objects where the investor believes that local actors are not aware of all the economically relevant characteristic of the property. Some years ago, a Swedish real estate fund came to believe that brown properties that were easy to make green were 'underpriced'. Their strategy was to buy these buildings, transform them to green buildings and then sell the buildings and make a nice profit. The fund was very opportunistic when choosing what green certificate to aim at. If the building had a 'good' location from a sustainability perspective, they aimed at broader classification system, but if the building had a 'bad' location, then they aimed at a certificate that only focused on the quality of the building as such. Another example is that international investors in the late 1990s realized that the Swedish market did not take the length of the rental contract and the characteristic of the tenant into account. The investor focused on buying underpriced properties with long contracts and financially strong tenants, calculating that the market would soon realize that these properties had a higher value and then they could sell with a profit.

7.6 Concluding Comments

As mentioned in Section 7.1, we will return to the more general challenges that sustainability and climate change has for the valuation profession in Chapter 9 on governance and ethics. The discussion in this chapter has to a large extent focused on commercial buildings, but similar issues are relevant for apartments and single-family houses. A large number of studies have investigated the relation between environmental characteristics and prices on the housing market. Similar issues as the ones discussed above are covered: Are prices only reflecting the direct benefit in terms of lower heating costs or are there also an extra premium from the greenness as such? The results in Aroul and Rodriguez (2017) indicate that the importance of the green characteristic for price has grown over time.

It should, however, be remembered that in the end it is an empirical question how much environmental and green aspects influence market values. Robinson and Singh (2019) find that net operating income is lower for green hotels as operating costs increase more than revenue and Robinson and McAllister (2015) find no significant value differences for offices in some larger UK markets. As property values to a large extent depend on expectations and beliefs and as these differ between markets, it should not be surprising that the green premium also varies.

From a valuation perspective, climate change and sustainability aspects create new risks that need to be evaluated for investors (see, e.g. Hirsch et al. 2015). The risks concern climate change as such – how quick will the changes be, exactly what form will they take in the specific local market. But the risk also concerns the policy responses to these changes, e.g. changes in tax system or in the transportation system. These risks can have large effects on property value, especially in some locations and especially where there have been dramatic weather events.

Exercises

1 What environmental classification systems dominate in your local market? Are there local environmental classification systems beside the international ones? How do the systems differ? How costly is it to reach a higher level? Is there a pattern among property owners concerning who uses a certain system?

2 How large role does sustainability play on your local market? Are certain aspects given more weight than others? How large share of new construction in different segments are classified?

3 How do local valuers take climate change and other environmental factors into account? What methods are used and how are they adjusted to incorporate these factors?

4 How do different actors take environmental aspects into account when they calculate their investment values? Are there certain actors that are more interested in investing in green buildings than others?

5 How are banks evaluating green buildings? Are financing opportunities better for green buildings through green bonds?

8

Transparency Issues

Discussions about transparency concern both the real estate market and the transparency of the property valuations.

8.1 Transparent and Rational Markets

8.1.1 Historical Background

After a downturn on the real estate or stock market, the transparency of the market is often discussed. This can, for example, concern a crash on foreign markets where investors lost money. In the aftermath to the economic crisis in South East Asia 1997, one explanation for the losses was that foreign investors had been misled and that the market had not been transparent enough. The lesson was that if a country wanted to attract foreign investments, it should create a higher level of transparency.[1]

After the corporate scandals in the early 2000s that involved companies like WorldCom and Enron, there was also a discussion about transparency in company reports. In these cases, the company reports had been seriously misleading and overstated profits and financial positions dramatically. These scandals therefore had consequences for the auditing profession and rules for auditing firms.

In a similar way, there were discussions after the financial crises in 2008–2009, especially about some new and very complex financial instruments. The argument was that this lack of transparency had led to an underestimation of the risk in these investments with overpricing and later a crash in the value of these assets as a result. An example is the following statement in *The Appraisal of Real Estate* (2013), p. 132–133:

---

1 The results presented in Saduyaki et al. (2019) are, however, mixed on this point.

Advanced Issues in Property Valuation, First Edition. Hans Lind and Bo Nordlund.
© 2021 John Wiley & Sons Ltd. Published 2021 by John Wiley & Sons Ltd.

The market forces that increased the efficiency of real estate markets and liquidity of real estate investments also reduced the transparency of the assets pooled in heavily traded securitized mortgage instruments, obscuring the risk involved in holding the loans that backed those securities from buyers.

In the wake of the housing crisis of 2007–2008, transparency in real estate markets has become a significant concern of market observers just as it was in the aftermath of real estate downturns in 1988–1989 and 1999–2000.

8.1.2 JLL's Transparency Index

The consultancy firm JLL has during the last 20 years regularly published a report on the transparency of real estate market where different countries are compared. It can be seen as a reaction to the transparency problems around the year 2000 described above. This section is based on the report in 2018 (JLL 2018), a report that really can be recommended if one wants to have a deeper knowledge about what is happening in different parts of the world with respect to transparency.

Transparency is in the report measured by looking at six subindices that are presented below. All in all, 186 individual questions and data points are used to construct the index. In recent years, they have also added a special subindex that describes the market from a sustainability point of view.

1) *Performance measurement*
   In a highly transparent market, there should be indices with returns to direct property investments, but also indices for real estate securities and private real estate funds. The quality of valuations is also part of this group of transparency measures.
2) *Market fundamentals*
   Are there data on rents, operating costs and vacancies on different submarkets: offices, retail, industrial, hotels and residential?
3) *Governance of listed vehicles*
   Here, the transparency on the company level is in focus: What is the quality of financial data disclosed? Is it easy to find out who owns and controls a real estate company?
4) *Regulatory and legal issues*
   How transparent and predictable is the tax system, the building codes and zoning regulations? How reliable and efficient is the land and property registration? This heading also covers rules concerning eminent domain, including compensation rules, and rules about property lending and foreclosure.

5) *The transaction process*

How easy is it to buy and sell properties? How are the sales process organized? How predictable is the process? JLL also includes the availability of occupier services in this subindex.

6) *Sustainability*

Are green building certificates available on the market? Do green leases exist? Are there energy benchmarking and efficiency standards? Is information available on carbon footprint and financial performance of green buildings?

Table 8.1 shows part of the results.

Constructing a transparency index does, however, include a number of decisions that are not uncontroversial. Exactly which factors should be included? How should the different factors be weighed against each other? How should each factor be measured? How is the quality of the data that is used to construct a certain index? Is it really better with an index with data of low quality than no index at all? An example illustrating these problems is that ever since the first transparency index was constructed, real estate specialists in Sweden have complained that the country deserves a higher ranking. They also complain that it is not transparent enough how the transparency index is constructed and how each dimension is measured.

Table 8.1 Most transparent countries 2018.

Category	Global rank	Market	Score
Highly transparent	1	United Kingdom	1.24
	2	Australia	1.32
	3	United States	1.37
	4	France	1.44
	5	Canada	1.45
	6	Netherlands	1.51
	7	New Zealand	1.59
	8	Germany	1.88
	9	Ireland	1.93
	10	Sweden	1.93
	11	Finland	1.95
Transparent	12	Singapore	1.97
	13	Hong Kong	1.97
	14	Japan	1.98

8.1.3 An Example of an Organization That Really Tries to Be Transparent

The Swedish central bank (The Riksbank) has during the last 25 years had a clear policy with transparency in focus. The underlying idea is that the more predictable the central bank is, the more it will contribute to stabilizing the economy. By looking at their strategy, it also becomes clearer why there are limits to transparency in the private sector.

The first part of the transparency policy of the Riksbank is to regularly publish reports that give their view of the national and global situation. The reports present their analysis of recent events and more long-term trends. Twice a year they publish a 'Monetary policy report' (earlier called 'Inflation report') and a 'Financial stability report'.

Policy decisions are taken by an Executive Board with six members, and the minutes of their meetings are made public including detailed information about how each member of the board voted and why. The most important of these decisions are the determination in their interest rate (the repo rate). Knowing if the vote was 6-0 or 3-3 (with the Governor having the deciding vote) gives information about what might happen the next time they meet.

All members of the executive board are very publicly active with lectures and participation in seminars. Together they participate in around 20 such events every year. The idea is that in this way they can also present the view of the central bank continuously and comment on recent events. However, they are seldom ready to give answers to surprising and important questions from the audience when giving these lectures if answers on such questions could be interpreted as giving new important information to the market.

The final part of the transparency policy is that they publish a prediction of the future central bank interest rate. In that way they can signal if they think that the interest rate rather soon will rise or not? Even if the Riksbank did not change the repo rate when the corona pandemic started early in 2020, they changed their prediction and said that it would probably take a long time before they would increase the interest rate. After the meeting in September 2020, they said that the zero interest can be expected to continue three more years.

All this means that when the Riksbank changes the interest rate, it is already expected by actors on the market and do not upset the market.

8.1.4 How Transparent Can a Market Be?

If we first look at transparency from the perspective of a single company, it is obvious that no company can be as transparent as the Swedish Riksbank. A company cannot give detailed information about how top management thinks about various events and about the plans of the company concerning future products and prices. Such information can be used by competitors and would give the competitors an advantage. A lot of things are judged to be 'business secrets'.

There are some interesting exceptions in situations where all parties realize that the sector as a whole gains if they share information. Such information sharing can be about vacancies and room rates in the hotel sector. Such information sharing makes it possible for participants to identify what are the general changes on the market and what are the changes in their relative attractiveness. Another example is exchange of technical information and licensing of the use of technologies in the car industry. The availability of real estate indices, captured from individual firms who supply data on, say, rents, and operating costs is another example which can help the participants gain confidence that gains for the sector as a whole are larger than losses related to better-informed competitors. Typically, the participating firms only get aggregate information back, but well-informed actors can probably draw conclusions from these about the situation of the larger competitors. As the real estate market competes with stocks and bonds, and as these investment classes in some respect are seen as more transparent, it has become important also for companies in the real estate sector to increase transparency, even if it comes with a cost.

A conclusion from this is that discussions about transparency need to take into account some basic features of a market economy. Nobel laureate von Hayek wrote a famous article called 'The use of information in society' (Hayek 1945). One central argument was that in a market economy - compared to a planned economy - there are strong incentives for actors to collect and use local information, as this information can be used for economic gains. When information is valuable for actors on the market, it cannot be assumed that they are willing to share this information. An investment company that has understood that a certain submarket is undervalued or overvalued in relation to the information it has will use this information to its advantage and not share it. A consulting firm that collects more and better data has a comparative advantage in relation to other firms and it cannot be expected that it is willing to present this information in a way that competitors use. Of course, firms will monitor the behaviour of others and try to draw conclusion from observed behaviour about what the other firms might know - but the behaviour of a company can also be a way of trying to mislead others.

If actors are assumed to be self-interested, there can also be incentives to misreport and in various ways send wrong signals to the market. Here are some examples:

- For tax reasons, the reported transaction price might be lower than the true one.
- A company that sells a property might not want to report a loss and therefore try to increase the price by, for example, giving a loan with generous conditions or give rent guarantees. These side-conditions might be secret and only known to a small group of people.

- Similar actions can be found on the rental market for offices. Instead of reducing the rent level in a recession, an initial rent-free period can be agreed on. During a recession, the property owner might be willing to renovate the property at their own expense, but during the boom, the tenant will have to pay this cost. This means that reported rents fluctuate less than the underlying real rent. If it is important to keep up the reported rent level, there are also incentives to choose vacancy instead of reducing the rent in order to find a tenant. Lowering the rent may, for example, lead to other tenants demanding reduced rents.

All this creates challenges for authorities and organizations that want to create a more transparent market, e.g. creating indices for property returns and rents. From a valuation perspective, it shows how important it really is to have 'an ear to the ground' and follow market movements and the strategies of self-interested managers.

8.2 Transparent Valuation Reports

Another aspect of transparency concerns the valuation process and valuation reports. IVCS (2019, p. 1 and 6) underlines the importance of transparency:

> The International Valuation Standards (IVS) are standards for undertaking valuation assignments using generally recognised concepts and principles that promote transparency and consistency in valuation practice.
>
> For a valuation to be credible, it is important that those judgements are made in a way that promotes transparency and minimises the influence of any subjective factors on the process. Judgement used in a valuation must be applied objectively to avoid biased analyses, opinions and conclusions.

In *The Appraisal of real estate* (2013, p. 101), one can read:

> In recent years, the clients of appraisers have spearheaded the movement toward uniform data standards by demanding more consistency, efficiency, and transparency within the appraisal process.

RICS (2019, p. 53) makes this somewhat more precise by requiring that the valuers describe the approach used, the key inputs and the principal reasons for the conclusions reached.

For a report to be transparent, one could demand the following:

- Clearness about the value concept, and as discussed in Chapter 2, it might be necessary to comment on underlying assumptions about turnover on the market as the expected price depends on expected turnover.

- Clearness about the valuation method. As discussed in Chapter 3, the lines between sales comparison methods and income methods can be drawn in different ways. If several methods have been used, it is important to clarify how independently they have been used. Adjustment methods should also be presented.
- Sources and quality of the underlying data. It has been argued that one way to make valuations more transparent is to demand that the valuer presents the observed transactions that are judged to be most relevant for the conclusion about the market value.
- The arguments that led from the data and the results from using the method (methods) to the final conclusion about the value.
- A discussion about how uncertain the result is. How different degrees of uncertainty can be presented was discussed in Chapter 4.

There are, however, several challenges when valuation reports should be made transparent.

As mentioned above, the raw data available may in different ways be misleading and the valuation company may have informal information about rent-free periods or various discounts and side-conditions. As mentioned above, information about recent transactions is information that can give a consultancy firm a competitive advantage and they can be expected to be reluctant to present more detailed information about these transactions. But, in order to make valuations more transparent, some information of this type has to be presented.

Relevant information about what is going on in the market and especially the most recent trends that can be expected to come from more informal sources might be difficult for the valuer to disclose. When more actor-based methods are used – see Chapter 3 - and the valuer uses information about how participants in bidding and transactions have calculated and argued, it can also be difficult to be precise about sources. The information may be business secrets, or be information that the valuers will not get in the future if they give away their current sources.

Valuation is sometimes called an art and not a science. One interpretation of this is that the valuer uses experience and tacit knowledge when estimating the probable price. What this means has been investigated in Amidu et al. (2019a).[2] They summarize their results as follows:

> However, through studying cognitive processes, it was demonstrated that meta-reasoning enables expert valuers to utilise their extensive domain-specific knowledge to manage efficiently the valuation task

---

2 See also Amidu and Boyd (2018) and Amidu et al. (2019a,b).

making selections and balance multiple sources and qualities of data. This makes it look easy, but the sophisticated meta-reasoning determines the reasoning effort that is put into various tasks and the balance between experiential and theoretical knowledge processes. (p. 535)

An experienced valuer has built up knowledge about how people in the market think and what data are reliable and when to be suspicious. It can be knowledge about professional investors on the commercial real estate market, but also about general preferences among buyers of apartments and houses of different types. This knowledge has been built up over years and cannot easily be described, and the valuer may not be able to specify more in detail what these beliefs are based on. If tacit knowledge plays a role in valuations, it poses challenges to making valuation reports very transparent. In many areas in society, there is a demand for evidence-based policies/treatments/statements and relying much on 'experience' will then be seen as problematic. On the other hand, not using this experience could lead to valuations with lower quality. The study mentioned above also shows that there are a number of steps where 'intuition' is not really in conflict with verifiable procedures. Sometimes, intuition just makes the process more efficient.

8.3 Concluding Comments

One conclusion from this chapter is that transparency is important both on the market and in valuation reports, but that there are limits to transparency both on the real estate market as such and in the process that determines the market value of a property. Information has value that gives a competitive edge in both cases, and actors may not disclose more than is absolutely necessary for the purpose at hand. Actors can also be expected to be more open with information that is to their own advantage.

Given the importance of market data for valuations it is very important that reliable data about transactions are available. Information should for example be presented about underlying property values when properties are sold as companies (wrappers), about side-conditions and relevant tax information should also be presented (see chapter 3).

A complementary mechanism to transparency is certification and reputation. The estimated value might be seen as reliable not because it has been reached by a transparent process, but because the valuation is carried out by a certified valuer that works for a firm with a good reputation. For such a valuer and for such a firm, it would simply be too risky to be partial and present a biased valuation. This leads to questions discussed in the next chapter on governance and ethics.

Exercises

1 How is your country ranked from a transparency perspective? Do you think the ranking is fair?

2 Looking at the local market – what information is available? Can it be trusted? What would be the most important thing to do in order to make it more transparent?

3 Look at local property valuations: How transparent are they in different dimensions? Can the steps in the valuation be followed? What could be improved?

4 Pro and con: Is high market transparency a reasonable goal in a market economy?

5 Pro and con: Is high transparency a reasonable goal for property valuations?

9

Valuation Ethics, the Role of the Valuer and Governance

9.1 The Importance of Valuation and Basic Ethical Rules

Valuation is important for society, not least for lending decisions and therefore also for the working of the financial system. This means that society has an interest in both a well-functioning property market, and that valuations are carried out in a professional way following basic ethical rules. An early example is the Swedish ordinances from the eighteenth century that stipulates that valuations for bank lending should be carried out by two persons appointed by the Magistrate/Mayor. There were regulations concerning loan-to-value ratios but also about valuation methods, where it was stipulated that a net capitalization method should be used. As mentioned in Chapter 5, minimum yield rates were also regulated in these ordinances.

In both RICS Red Book (RICS 2019, p. 18f) and *The Appraisal of Real Estate* (2013, p. 718), basic ethical rules are formulated. These include, for example, that the valuer should

- be impartial and objective
- avoid conflict of interest
- only accept assignments when they have the necessary skill
- not disclose confidential information.

RICS (2012) also underline the importance of what they call professional scepticism: the valuer should not use data and other kinds of information without checking the reliability of the data. This is, of course, especially important when data are supplied by a party that has certain interest: see the earlier section on client influence in Chapter 4.

Ethical rules also concern companies, for example, that the company should have a strict separation between advisors working for clients with conflicting

Advanced Issues in Property Valuation, First Edition. Hans Lind and Bo Nordlund.
© 2021 John Wiley & Sons Ltd. Published 2021 by John Wiley & Sons Ltd.

interests (RICS 2012, p. 22) and a rotation of valuers when the valuation company has provided a series of valuations for a longer time (p. 25).

In order to uphold such fundamental rules, some form of governance and supervision is needed and various ways to do that is discussed in Section 9.3. But, first it is necessary to discuss the role of the valuer.

9.2 The Responsibility of Valuers and Valuation Firms

The role of the valuer should also be discussed from a broader perspective. Should the valuer just reflect the market as it is, or also has a broader responsibility in relation to the development of society? During the last 30 years, this issue has been raised in at least two specific contexts.

9.2.1 Property Crises

The first situation was after crises around 1990, where the main issue was whether the valuers or their organizations should have issued some kind of warning when the boom got more extreme? In the book *Value in a Changing Built Environment* (Lorenz et al. 2019), they argue that:

> While cycles of boom and bust occur, the property profession can do a lot to make them less damaging. (p. 9)

This is very much related to valuation concepts and risk analysis as discussed in earlier chapters. Possible proposals in this context is that risk analysis should be extended, e.g. in the ways discussed in Chapter 4. Evaluating risk is, however, very difficult and many crises have occurred in new situations where risks were very difficult to estimate. During the typical boom, most actors are optimistic and do not take those who talk about risk seriously and point out that they have warned a number of times when no crisis actually occurred.

Another proposal is that beside information about market value, there should be information about alternative value concepts like mortgage lending value and/or worth (investment value). This was discussed more in detail in Chapter 4. An advantage with these strategies is that it is not expected that anyone has better information about the future than 'the market' or that risk can be measured in some relatively objective way.

For reasons discussed in Section 9.3 on governance, it can be problematic for a single valuer or a single valuation firm to do things that are not in line with the interest of the client and/or the current state or sentiment of the market and the actors being active there. It is therefore especially important that governing bodies are active on these issues.

9.2.2 Sustainability

During the last decades, climate change and other environmental issues have more and more come to the centre of the debates in society: warmer climate, higher sea level and more extreme weather are discussed at all levels of society. It is also clear that these changes, and policies related to them, will affect the property market and property values in a number of ways as was discussed in the last chapter.

Lorenz et al. (2019)[1] strongly argue that the valuer has a broader role in relation to sustainability. Their general standpoint is summarized as follows:

> The valuation exercise is not only a positive science; that is to say, valuers are not only here to 'reflect the market'. Instead, valuers have a normative professional responsibility towards society at large. (p. 4)
>
> Specifically for the valuer, as a professional adviser, the ethics of sustainable solutions should form an important part of any appraisal and judgement when advising a client. (p. 5)
>
> The professions could, and probably should, take a lead in addressing both the technical fix and the behavioural shift needed to mitigate both the impacts of climate change and the loss of important and valued public goods. (p. 177)

RICS (2012) are less radical and write

> While valuers should reflect markets, not lead them, they should be aware of sustainability features and the implications these could have on property values in the short, medium and longer term. (p. 5)

RICS also underline that in order to comply with best practice, valuers should enhance their knowledge of sustainability issues. They should collect data about sustainability characteristics and also be able to evaluate sustainability-related property characteristics in the relation to sustainability criteria. RICS encourage valuers to gather environmentally relevant information and that they present a Sustainability Check List in their report.

One can imagine that a supervising authority issues more or less binding directives that certain information should be presented, like the sustainability check list from RICS. This could of course also include demands concerning alternative value concepts or standardized reports about uncertainty.

---

1 See also Hill et al. (2013).

More and more companies and organization have sustainability policies and policies related to corporate social responsibility. This is true both for real estate companies and real estate consultancies. In the boxes below, there are some examples from Sweden.

Example 9.1   The Real Estate Company Vasakronan

https://vasakronan.se/en/about-vasakronan/sustainability/our-responsibility/

> Our sustainability initiatives are based on a framework comprised of the *UN Global Compact*; 10 principles aimed at companies and concerning human rights, labour, environment and anti-corruption. We also base our efforts on the UN Sustainable Development Goals and have identified the goals that are material for our operations. We have two codes of conduct – one for employees and one for suppliers – which our employees and suppliers are required to follow. We also have an environmental policy that applies to all employees at Vasakronan.

Example 9.2   The Property Advisor JLL

https://www.jllsweden.se/en/about-jll/our-sustainability-leadership

> Together with our partners we aim to drive disruptive and impactful change by embedding sustainability into everything we do. By helping you take a responsible and sustainable approach that contributes to a better world, we are working to shape the future of real estate.

Example 9.3   SVEFA (A Company That Has Property Valuation as One Core Business)

> Our quality and environmental policy: We shall through our professionality, integrity and commitment create value as real estate consultants. We shall in a goal oriented ways work for continuous improvement of our work and reduce our negative impact on the environment, and make sure that we fulfill the demands of our clients. When carrying out our services we shall aim at illustrating preconditions for protecting the environment and successively improve our environmental performance.

The dichotomy between reflecting the market and leading the market becomes less clear and relevant in a situation where the market is very heterogenous and many actors have sustainability policies. On a market where there are real estate companies and real estate investors who take environmental goals seriously, it is obvious that a professional valuer and a professional valuation company need be knowledgeable about sustainability issues.

A heterogenous market is, however, also a market where there are laggards and less serious actors, e.g. that want to hide environmental problems in a property and who wants to find valuers that they can put pressure on. There is always a risk for a 'race to the bottom' in an unregulated market with asymmetric information. This makes the question of authorization/certification very important for keeping a high level of quality and integrity in the valuation profession.

9.3 Authorization/Certification of Valuers

Markets are often characterized by asymmetric information. Authorization is one way to reduce some of the problems caused by asymmetric information.

Consumer protection is one argument for some kind of authorization of professionals. An example is that in Sweden, real estate brokers that work with residential housing that is bought and sold by ordinary households (single-family houses and apartments) must be authorized by the state. No such authorization is needed for brokers that work with commercial properties. The argument for this is that households seldom buy or sell properties and that properties have high values. Therefore, there is a clear risk that some households will be misled by a partial or incompetent broker. Companies are assumed to be better at protecting their own interests and therefore authorization should not be needed for brokers on the commercial market.

After the dramatic real estate and banking crises in Sweden in the early 1990s, the reputation of property valuers was low, and the property industry contacted the government in order to establish an authorization system for property valuers. The government said no and argued that the industry could establish and administer a (voluntary) authorization system themselves. The explanation was probably that such an authorization was not important from a consumer protection perspective as valuers seldom are hired by private households. This is even more true today when various automatic valuation models for single-family homes are common. Simple valuations of a house or an apartment are now available free of charge on websites of both brokers and banks.

The interest from an industry in a voluntary authorization system can be explained by Akerlofs 'Market for lemons' argument (Akerlof 1970). In a market with incomplete information, where buyers cannot easily distinguish higher quality from lower quality, there might be a 'race to the bottom'. It might be difficult for those who deliver higher quality to set a higher price, when the buyer has difficulties in knowing if there really is a higher quality. Those who deliver a higher quality can therefore be interested in a voluntary authorization system that makes it possible for them to signal that they have higher quality.

Besides improving the information on a market, an authorization system also changes the incentive structure. It can be easier to punish those who deliver bad services if there is an authorization system. The Swedish system for authorization of (housing) brokers can illustrate this point. If a buyer or seller is dissatisfied with a broker, they can file a complaint at The Swedish Estate Agents Inspectorate. The inspectorate can issue warnings but can also withdraw the authorization. For a dissatisfied customer, it is much easier to send a complaint to a government authority – or a professional organization - than going to court. Usually it does not cost anything to file a complaint. An authorization system can also make it easier for a valuer to withstand client pressure as the cost of being partial is higher when the valuer might lose their authorization if they do what the client wants (see, e.g. Małkowska et al. 2019). Another example of public institutions for surveillance/monitoring and disciplinary routines can be found for auditors and auditing firms. These rules have been made more stringent after the company scandals mentioned above.

Authorization systems differ in at least two dimensions: whether they are mandatory or voluntary and whether they are run by the government or by some independent industry organizations. This gives four options, illustrated in Table 9.1. In the rest of this section, the focus will be on type 1 - mandatory government systems - and type 4 - voluntary industry organized systems.

There are important arguments for authorization system related to asymmetric information, but there are also problems. A mandatory authorization system creates a monopoly and can be used to reduce supply and thereby increase incomes for those with authorization. The crucial issue is the rules for authorization. These rules typically include both that the person should have a certain level of education and that they have experience from working in the business, e.g. as an assistant to an authorized person. It is not an easy question to decide the necessary level of education (and the necessary content of the education) and the types of

Table 9.1 Different types of authorization systems.

	Mandatory	Voluntary
By government	1	2
By industry	3	4

experience needed. Those who have an authorization and those who have a certain higher education typically argue that a rather high level of education is needed.

A voluntary system may have another problem. Raising the demands for an authorization may lead to a situation where many choose to stand outside the system. As the voluntary system typically is run by people active in the field, the organization may also be reluctant to introduce demands that might not be good for their business, at least not in the short run. An example: as discussed in Chapter 4, after a crash on the market, there are typically discussions about uncertainty in valuations. Should the organization introduce a demand that authorized valuers must discuss uncertainty in a structured way? Our impression is that in the end, not much is done. When the market turns up again, the issue of uncertainty is forgotten until the next crash. Even if it would be good for the profession and the market in the long run that such discussions were introduced, the potential negative short run effects might be given more weight – if those who pay for valuations are not interested in discussions of uncertainty. An authorization system run by a voluntary organization might therefore be rather conservative when it comes to introducing rules that should increase the quality of the valuation from a long-term perspective, e.g. concerning sustainability.

The German system with mortgage lending value and regulated valuation methods can be seen as a questioning of the market's possibility to regulate itself. It might be difficult for actors on the market to go against the tide when there is a boom on the market and where actors - partly using other peoples' money - are willing to pay (too) high amounts for properties. More direct government action to regulate a profession like valuers may also be more necessary in earlier stages of the development of a country where organizations are weaker. The Swedish ordinances from the eighteenth century mentioned above is an example of this.

9.4   Concluding Comments

In a market, there is a constant struggle between serious actors who want to make profits by producing price-worthy goods and services, and those who in one way or the other plan to make money by cheating or by using rules and regulations to their own advantage. Governance issues are therefore very important and professional organizations and authorization systems can both improve information and change incentives in the right direction. History, however, also shows that such organization and regulations can be used to further the interest of a small group, and it is therefore important to be somewhat sceptical. What RICS called 'professional scepticism' is important also in this context.

There are rather rapid changes in the areas discussed in this chapter. Sustainability policies, governance issues and policies related to Corporate social responsibility are now often discussed together under the heading ESG (environment, social and governance). Various standards have been formulated, e.g. Global Reporting Initiative (www.globalreporting.org) and Sustainability Accounting Standards Board (https://www.sasb.org/). Earlier, we mentioned the MSCI-ESG standard for the real estate sector (https://www.msci.com/esg-ratings).

Exercises

1   Look at the ethical rules of local organizations for valuers. What is your opinion about the clarity and relevance of these rules?

2   What are the role of the government and the role of professional organizations for governing valuations in your local market? What are the views of clients and the valuers about the current situation?

3   Has there in your local market been cases where valuers have been criticized for acting unethically or have been taken to court? What happened in these cases and do they indicate that there is a need for change in the governance system? Discuss: What has been questioned and what was paid attention to in the verdict? Formal things as reported rentable square metres or other kinds of building descriptions, or maybe what is allowed for use by legislation for a certain property? Or is the reported value figure (e.g. estimated market value) questioned (too high or too low)?

4   Pro and con: Should the government regulate and supervise the valuation sector harder? What should – should not – be regulated in such a case?

5   Pro and con: Should the valuer have broader responsibility to contribute to a more sustainable society? What would that imply in practice?

10

Property Valuation in the Future

Three aspects will be discussed briefly in this chapter: Technological developments, structural changes caused by unexpected events – exemplified by the corona-pandemic 2020 – and finally, the issue of 'radical uncertainty'. As we all know, discussing the future is a risky and uncertain enterprise and the reader of this book will probably see that some of the things said below will already be outdated!

10.1 Technological Development

> Looking ahead, new technologies promise the next 'leap' in transparency, with the prospect that our ability to harness 'big data' and digital platforms will revolutionise the sector.
>
> (JLL 2018)

10.1.1 Big Data and Data Collection

New kinds of data are increasingly being used for analysing, e.g. the attractiveness of an area or trends on the market. This can be say, data on movements based on mobile phones to analyse the attractiveness of retail locations. Textual analysis or studying search words can be used to measure sentiment. Examples of such studies are de DeLisle et al. (2020) who discuss Big Data in general, Guo et al. (2020) who try to capture market sentiment from text mining and Braun (2016) who uses search data from Google.

Advanced Issues in Property Valuation, First Edition. Hans Lind and Bo Nordlund.
© 2021 John Wiley & Sons Ltd. Published 2021 by John Wiley & Sons Ltd.

More and more data on buildings are also available in real time, e.g. energy use in a building. Drones are also used to collect data for property valuation, especially when agricultural and forest properties are valued or for mapping the environment around a property to be valued.

10.1.2   AI

Big data are not very useful unless they are analysed. Using Artificial Intelligence (AI) to analyse data is becoming more and more common. A main difference between the typical hedonic study of property prices (with regression analysis) and artificial intelligence methods is that the first type of model is based on a theory about what affects prices. The typical AI model starts with a more general mathematical structure and then 'trains' the model with existing data and then the model that works best on these data is used for predicting. The model is continuously updated when new data arrive. There are some academic studies comparing the results from traditional AI models and hedonic studies, e.g. Valier (2020).

10.1.3   The Demand for Valuers

Automatic valuations methods have in some countries taken over most valuations of single-family houses and apartments. Some actors believe that more and more of commercial valuations will also be done by automatic methods and that the demand for valuers will fall over time.

Others draw a parallel to the development in the car industry: maybe self-driving cars are a long way off, but the driver step by step gets help from more and more advanced warning systems, automatic brakes and automatic anti-sliding system. In a similar way, a number of automatic systems will help the valuer of commercial buildings and make preliminary valuations given the data in the system, but the valuer is still needed to analyse the suggestions of the automatic system and make the final valuation (see Tajani et al. 2020). One can draw a parallel to how experts in authorities work with predicting the development of the economy: They have advanced economic models, but in the end, a group of experts evaluate the credibility of the results of the models and make the final decision about the prediction.

In the context of expert systems versus valuers, it is also important to underline the quality of data used in a model. In Chapter 6, for instance, we discussed the perceptions of free cash flows generated from property investments. We stressed the fact that on many occasions the user of financial statements needs to go beyond the income statement figures to find out the free cash flows of a property company. If net operating incomes are extracted only from information in income statements, this could on many occasions overstate the cash flow capacity. If such figures then are used in expert-systems or models when making valuations, such procedures could feed bubbles in the market.

10.1.4 Some Reservations

In a market with heterogenous properties, a continuously changing economy and a relatively low turnover, there will never be enough data to construct a model that is obviously superior to other models. Changes in the economy means that one cannot assume that relations are stable – and then one has to model these changes and then more data are needed. We discussed this in Chapter 3 that in a situation like this, it could be rational to use a limited number of 'most similar properties' when doing a valuation instead of using a statistical analysis.

Another problem is of course the quality of the data. We know from history that people have been very creative in manipulating data to further their own interest, e.g. data from companies about rents and operating cost as discussed in earlier chapters. Checking data can partly also be automatized, but it should be expected that there will be a continuous struggle between those who want to make the system reliable and those who want to manipulate the system. It will be difficult for users to know who has the upper hand.

There is also a problem with transparency perspective in the use of AI-systems, e.g. discussed in Valier (2020). These systems are like a black box. The algorithm may, after suitable training, be very good at predicting transaction prices, but the prediction cannot be explained in relation to various fundamental factors as when ordinary regression analysis is used in automated valuation systems. The information that has been put into the system can be described, but not the relation between these inputs and the final estimation of the market value. The mathematics used is too complex for non-experts to understand. This can reduce the credibility of the models as the user may want to know how the value was arrived at.

In economics, there has been a long discussion on a similar issue after Milton Friedman (1953) argued that a theory should be evaluated by its prediction and that the realism of the assumptions in the theory – e.g. rational consumer and profit maximizing companies – were irrelevant. One counterargument was that we want to understand how the prediction was arrived at and not only the outcome/results of 'the black box'. But such attitudes may of course change over time if the black box predictions really are very successful!

10.2   Structural Changes in Society: Corona-Pandemic as an Example

In earlier chapters, we discussed possible effects of climate change. The current corona-pandemic can illustrate how unexpected events can start or strengthen structural changes on the real estate market. It is of course too early to know what the actual effects will be but there are a number of possible structural changes on the real estate market:

- Many firms have realized that it is possible for employees to work from home. Will this lead to falling demand for offices in the future, if perhaps employees work from home at least one or two days a week? Co-working solutions can also be interesting instead of having an office of their own, especially for smaller firms.
- But if people work from home, then it should affect the demand for housing. More space would be needed in order to be able to work from home in a satisfactory way. The importance of the qualities of housing may also increase if people will travel less. The pandemic and environmental policies that increase the cost of travel could cause a change in behaviour. An example is that the demand for summer houses close to metropolitan areas increased considerably in Sweden during the spring of 2020.
- When more and more people get used to have meetings and conferences through digital platforms, companies and organizations might realize that at least a share of earlier meetings and conferences could be carried out through digital tools also in the future. If these tools are developed, they may be more and more competitive and lead to falling demand for hotels and conference facilities. Environmental considerations and time savings could pull in the same direction.
- Even before the pandemic, many shopping centres had economic problems caused by increasing internet shopping. Restrictions and recommendations during the pandemic increased internet shopping, especially among older households. Once households get used to this kind of shopping, they might continue even when the pandemic is over.

In a 'Practice paper', French (2020) discusses the covid-19 pandemic from the perspective of uncertainty in property valuations. Besides the general uncertainty that the pandemic creates, there are in many markets also fewer transactions to base valuations on. He writes:

> So, as with everything else in this strange new *COVID-19* world, valuations are inherently less certain and it is incumbent upon the valuer to let the client know that at the commencement of the instruction and to explain the uncertainties relating to the subject property and the market within it is being valued.

10.3   Radical Uncertainty and Property Valuation

The distinction between risk and uncertainty has sometimes been described as follows (see, e.g. King 2016):

> Risk is what can be quantified in models - the probability that it will occur and the effect if it does occur.

> Uncertainty is something that cannot be quantified in models in the same way as risk and assessment of this therefore requires elements of qualitative reasoning.

The book *Radical Uncertainty: Decision Making for an Unknowable Future'* (2020) written by the former governor of the Bank of England Mervyn King and the economist John Kay starts with a list of unexpected events – both economic and political. No one saw the coming of the financial crisis in 2008 and no one expected the terrorist attack on 11 September 2001. Before the wheel was invented by the Sumerians around 3500 B.C., there was no reasoning about the probability of such an invention and how this could affect the economy or the systems established. When the wheel was invented, this was new information that was incorporated in the perception of what was the new state of the world. Kay and King criticize the idea that uncertainty can be captured in mathematical models and underline that decision makers have to realize that there are a lot of things that we simply do not know and cannot know. They formulate three basic propositions.

1) The world of economics, business and finance is what they call non-stationary, i.e. there are no constant laws because the structure of the economy is always changing.
2) Evolutionary rationality: What is seen as rational is context-dependent. It is not possible to identify specific actions as in general more rational than others.
3) Humans are social animals: Humans tend to adapt their behaviour to what others do and what they expect others to do. There are tendencies to herd behaviour as discussed in Chapter 4.

A theory that can help to explain this 'radical uncertainty' is Chaos theory. The basic idea is that a small change in the initial characteristics of a system can lead to large differences in what happens in the system. An economy can be described as a complex system with many interacting parts and where relatively small differences in the characteristics of the system will affect how it will react to various changes. And these differences can be both how various firms and markets react and how the political system reacts.

The ideas about radical uncertainty can, however, be more important for investors than for property valuations. The more uncertain the situation is in the economy the more the value of a property would change over time and the riskier would the investment be. It should, however, not be forgotten that gut feelings and intuition always have been important for investors. The dispersion of prices in observed transaction would be higher if there are more uncertainties, but still the valuer could determine the most probable price at the current time, even if the risk for changes in this value is higher. If there is radical uncertainty, it would, however, not be possible to estimate how large these uncertainties are, and the kind of risk analysis described in Chapters 4 and 5 would be more problematic.

We recall discussions about property valuations in Sweden after the crisis in the early 1990s. Representatives of the banking sector said that they were more interested in the analysis presented in the valuation reports than the figure in the final paragraph – as they had learned how uncertain this figure was. The prediction was that the demand for standard property valuations would fall and be replaced by broader analysis of trends in the underlying markets. That would be a rational development if the world is felt to be more uncertain, but the prediction did not turn out to be correct.

One explanation for the return of the interest in property valuations were the new (questionable) accounting rules, where the market value of properties should be in the balance sheets and changes in values be reported in the income statements. Our impression is, however, also that ideas like those about radical uncertainty are discussed more when there has been a crisis of some type. When the economies are stabilized, again these ideas tend to fade and this is logical given that humans are social animal and find way to create a new picture of the situation and adjusting to this. As Kay and King (2020, p. 41) write 'Real households, real businesses and real governments do not optimize, they cope. They make decisions incrementally'.

Exercises

1   Pro and con: Will there be large structural changes as a result of the corona-pandemic and what might these be?

2   Pro and con: Have the uncertainty really increased? Will there soon be 'business as usual'?

3   Pro and con: Will there really be a market for standard property valuations in the future?

4 Discuss the distinction between risk and uncertainty. If all actors in a market really were aware of the uncertainty in future events, would required returns (e.g. yields) be higher? What is your perception of risk and uncertainty in the market where you work? How is risk/uncertainty assessed and has there been any changes recently, e.g. as a result of the corona-pandemic?

Appendix A

Can the Value of a Property Be Divided into Value of the Parts?

A.1 Introduction

Market value is typically estimated for objects that are bought and sold on a market. Sometimes, the question arises whether this value can be split into the value of different parts of the object sold. The most common such situation is that a house and the land that the house is built on is sold together – or at least that the house is sold together with a right to have a house on the land for the foreseeable future. The question then arises what the value of the building is and what the value of the land is. A similar case is the value of a farm, where you have a number of buildings, including a house for residential purposes, and agricultural land around these buildings. Can the value of the farm be divided into the value of the land and the value of the buildings? There have also been discussions about whether the whole value when, say, a shopping centre is sold is a property value or if part of the value instead should be seen as a 'business enterprise value'.

These questions arise in a number of contexts, e.g. if there are land-lease systems, where the fee should be adjusted over time in relation to the development of the land value. It can also be important for taxation purposes, where depreciation allowances only are allowed for the value of the building. Some countries only tax the value of the land and not the value of the buildings. If there is a property tax on commercial properties, then one could argue that the value that is taxed should not include the business enterprise value.

Advanced Issues in Property Valuation, First Edition. Hans Lind and Bo Nordlund.
© 2021 John Wiley & Sons Ltd. Published 2021 by John Wiley & Sons Ltd.

A.2 Dividing the Value into Land Value and Building Value for Homes and Commercial Buildings

A.2.1 Building Value as Residual

One strategy used in mass-valuation for taxation purposes, e.g. in Sweden, is that land is first valued separately, based on transactions of land only. The building value is then calculated as a residual - the difference between the estimated market value of the property as a whole and the estimated land value.

This residual value – called building value – cannot, however, be called the market value of the building as such. It is not the price that can be expected if the building was sold separately.

It is possible so sell the building separately in two ways. The owner might sell the building to someone who plans to disassemble the building and move it to some other place. This can be rational when the demand is low on the current market and where prices are high on some other market not far away – and where cost for disassembly, assembly and transportation is relatively low. But, there is no reason to believe that the sum of this building value and a market-derived land value equals the value of the property as a whole. In normal markets, it should be expected that the sum of the land value and the building value defined in this way is lower than the value of the property as a whole.

Another way to sell the building separately is to sell the building and a certain lease contract for the land. The buyer owns the building but not the land. But this approach does not give a unique building value as the expected price of the building to a large extent will be determined by the conditions in the lease contract.

Another serious problem with this strategy is how land values are estimated in a situation where no or very few lots are sold in built-up areas. The relation between price and turnover, as discussed in Chapter 2, means that the observed land prices can be expected to be much higher if only a few lots are coming out on the market. The market value as estimated from observed transactions will then be very unstable. In the Swedish land lease system, where the underlying land value should be updated every 20 years or so, there have been numerous court cases with very large differences in opinion between the parties about the size of the land value.

A.2.2 The Land Value as Residual

The problem with the first strategy is that in many built-up areas, there are very few or no land transactions. The alternative is then to calculate the land value as a residual. Strategy number two for dividing the total value into the land value and building value is then to start with the value of the property as a whole and then deduct a building value calculated as a depreciated replacement cost.

The logic behind this approach is clear. If there were vacant land and a known price for the property as a whole, the bid prices in a competitive market would be determined by this total value and the actors' estimation of the cost to complete the building. Mangioni (2015) describes the development of land taxation in Australia. Because of lack of land sales, there has been a move from the first method above to this second strategy.

As discussed in Chapter 3 in the context of valuation of development properties, this method is extremely sensitive to assumptions that are hard to verify. When a land value is determined as the difference between two large numbers, small changes in the estimation of the total value or in the estimation of the building cost will lead to large differences in the estimated value of the land.

A.2.3 Using Statistical Methods

A third way, discussed and used in Özdilek (2012, 2016), is to use statistical/hedonic methods. The starting point is then an assumption that the total value of the property is determined by the characteristics of the land and the characteristics of the building, and that these two factors are separable and that the sum of these values are equal to the whole. Statistical methods are then used to estimate the parameters that give the best fit. From these parameters, the total value can be divided into a land value and a building value.

The main problem with this strategy is the interpretation of the result: What kind of value is it really that the method gives? It is hard to see it as a division into the market value of the building and the market value of the land. The values are the result of assumptions – about separability and that the sum of the parts should equal the whole – and a statistical criterion – choose the parameters that give the best fit.

A.2.4 Dividing Property Values into Components for Accounting Purposes

The IFRS-accounting standard IAS 16 (2020) – Property, Plant & Equipment requires properties to be divided into parts (components) for depreciation purposes. Hence, properties in a first step need to be divided into values on land and building. The land-component will not be depreciated but the components of the building have to be identified and depreciated over their respective useful lives. This also means that values must be estimated for different parts (components) of the buildings and useful lives for each part have to be estimated. Davis and Wyndelts (1979) and Gilliland (1980) are examples of articles that discuss different views of splitting buildings into components for depreciation purposes. However, they discuss the issue primarily from a tax-rules perspective.

A.2.5 Conclusion

The conclusion of these arguments should be that it hardly is possible to divide the market value of a property consisting of a building and the land on which the building stands into a market value of the land, and a market value of the building that adds up to the market value of the property as a whole. By extension, this also means that it is hardly possible to divide buildings into components for depreciation purposes in the accounts and claim that the respective component's estimated values should be a market value/fair value. Some kind of mixed approach between entry and exit prices will probably be necessary to make such an estimation.

Because of administrative reasons, typically related to the accounting and tax system, there can be a need to identify a land value and a building value. For reasons given above, it is important not to call these values market value and the best might be to call them just administrative property values. As Mangioni (2015) discusses in the context of land taxation in Australia, when there is a lack of empirical evidence, the focus will be on the process used to arrive at the necessary values. The results are looked upon as fair if the procedure used is seen as fair. There is in most cases no way to test these values against the market in a consistent way.

A.3 Dividing the Value into Farmland and Farm Buildings

A typical farm consists of farmland and a number of buildings (including the land the buildings stand on), including the home of the farmer family. Often, this is sold as a whole when a new farmer family takes over the farm. Prices are observed for the complete package of residential house, buildings needed for farming, land that the building stands on and the farmland.

In this case, it is possible to sell the farmland and the buildings (including land) separately, especially if the farm is located close to metropolitan areas. The farmland would then be sold to neighbouring farms that want to increase the size of their business. They might be willing to pay a rather high price if they have excess capacity or if there are economies of scale. The buildings and the land that the buildings stand on would be sold to a non-farm household that plans to live there (or use it as a second home). The farm-related buildings might also be leased to neighbouring farms if the non-farm buyer does not want to use them for other purposes. In any case, there is a possible market for these parts and the market values for these parts could be estimated with standard methods.

In this case, there is, however, no reason to believe that the sum of these market values would equal the value of the property as a whole. The sum of the value of the parts can be higher if there is strong demand for farmland and for second homes in the area, but it can also be the other way around if it is a more remote and isolated location. It could be argued that if the sum of the value of the parts is higher than the value of whole property, then this would increase the value of the property as a whole as there is a valuable option to divide the farm into parts that could be sold separately. There might, however, be regulatory or cultural factors that work against splitting up the property and that could explain why it is sold as a whole even in situations where the sum of the value of the parts is higher.

Another way of thinking about the division of the farm value into value of land and value of buildings is to approach it in the same way as for residential and office properties – and with the same uncertainties as above. If the building value is seen as a residual, there is the problem with few pure land transactions. If the land value is seen as a residual, there is the problem of estimating construction cost and depreciation.

A.4   Dividing the Value into Property Value and 'Business Enterprise Value'

Let us think about an existing shopping centre with a number of running contracts and employed staff that manages the centre and makes decision about contracts, marketing and maintenance. To simplify the discussion, it is assumed that there is a company that owns and manages nothing but this shopping centre. The question then arises: What is the difference between selling the shopping centre property and selling the firm that owns the shopping centre? Can they be expected to fetch the same price on the market? To simplify further, it is assumed that there are no tax differences between buying the property and buying the firm, even though this is unrealistic in most countries.

Given these simplifications, and that rental contracts typically are valid even if the ownership of the property changes, the only difference between buying the property and buying the firm would be that in the latter case, the buyer also takes over the staff of the company.

There is no established definition of Business enterprise value, but one interpretation is that in a case like the one above, the Business enterprise value would be the difference between the market value of the firm and the market value of the property.

This, however, means that the Business enterprise value can be both positive and negative. If it is a well-managed shopping centre with a qualified and committed staff, then a buyer should be willing to pay more for the firm than for the property. On the other hand, if the centre is in rather poor shape and there is a need for rather drastic changes, then a buyer could prefer to start from scratch with completely new staff. The difference would also be affected by the labour laws in the country and the situation on the labour market. If it is easy and cheap to fire staff, it would not matter for a buyer whether they bought the firm or a company is in bad shape. The property and the firm would also have the same value even if it is a well-managed shopping centre and if it is judged to be easy to hire new qualified and committed staff.

In practice, it is very difficult to measure the difference between the value of the firm and the value of the property as companies typically have loans that have to be valued and that tax aspects will affect the price difference. There are also very few transactions that can be helpful in estimating this difference. If we demand that a meaningful concept is such that it is possible to measure with at least some precision, then it is questionable whether Business enterprise value is a meaningful concept.

A.5   Concluding Comment

There are two general lessons from this appendix. The first concerns conceptual clarity: What do we really talk about when we use concepts like the value of land and the value of a building for a built-up property? One conclusion should be that it cannot really be a market value if it concerns something that is not sold on a market.

The second point – illustrated by the short discussion about Business enterprise value – is the importance of being clear about what is included in a sale and what is not included. One can imagine situations where the buyer of a property in a side contract offers the current management staff to remain. It can also be the case that, say, a municipality that sells a portfolio of properties to a private company demands that the private company shall take over the staff that manages the properties. All these conditions will affect the observed price.

Exercises

1   Investigate if there are contexts in your local market where property values are divided into parts? Why is it done and what methods are used?

2   If a company is sold instead of the property – are there any tax rules that can cause the price to differ? Assume that there are no loans in the company.

References

Adair, A., Hutchison, N., MacGregor, B. et al. (1996). An analysis of valuation variation in the UK commercial property market. *Journal of Property Valuation & Investment* 14 (5): 34–48.

Ahn, J., Hoitash, R., and Hoitash, U. (2019). Auditor task-specific expertise: the case of fair value accounting. *Accounting Review, Forthcoming*. Avaliable at SSRN: https://ssrn.com/abstract=3192536 or http://dx.doi.org/10.2139/ssrn.3192536.

Akerlof, G.A. (1970). The market for "lemons": quality uncertainty and the market mechanism. *The Quarterly Journal of Economics* 84 (3): 488–500.

Amidu, A.-R. and Boyd, D. (2018). Expert problem solving practice in commercial property valuation: an exploratory study. *Journal of Property Investment & Finance* 36 (4): 366–382.

Amidu, A.-R., Boyd, D., and Agboola, A.O. (2019a). The role of knowledge in valuation practice: expert valuers' perceptions. *Journal of Property Investment & Finance* 37 (6): 524–540.

Amidu, A.-R., Boyd, D., and Gobet, F. (2019b). A study of the interplay between intuition and rationality in valuation decision making. *Journal of Property Research* 36 (4): 387–418. https://doi.org/10.1080/09599916.2019.1687572.

Anop-Engerstam, S. (2015). Apartment price determinants: a comparison between Sweden and Germany. Licentiate Thesis. KTH-Royal Institute of Technology.

Appraisal Institute (2013). *The Appraisal of Real Estate*, 14e. Chicago: Appraisal Institute.

Aroul, R.R. and Rodriguez, M. (2017). The increasing value of green for residential real estate. *Journal of Sustainable Real Estate* 9 (1): 112–130.

Baum, A. and Crosby, N. (2008). *Property Investment Appraisal*, 3e. Oxford: Blackwell Publishing.

Baum, A., Crosby, N., Gallimore, P. McAllister, P., and Gray, A. (2000). The influence of valuers and valuations on the workings of the commercial property investment market. *RICS, Cutting Edge Conference*, London.

Advanced Issues in Property Valuation, First Edition. Hans Lind and Bo Nordlund.
© 2021 John Wiley & Sons Ltd. Published 2021 by John Wiley & Sons Ltd.

Bélanger, P., Bourdeau-Brien, M., and Dumestre, M. (2018). The impact of flood zones on residential property prices: the case of Canada. *Journal of Sustainable Real Estate* 10 (1): 135–162.

Bellman, L. (2018). High-impact information types on market value: property appraisers' information sources and assessment confidence. *Journal of Property Research* https://doi.org/10.1080/09599916.2018.1443152.

Bellman, L. and Lind, H. (2018) Valuation standards and methods: are Sweden's (still) different?, *Journal of European Real Estate Research*, https://doi.org/10.1108/JERER-04-2018-0020.

Benston, G.J. (2008). The shortcomings of fair-value accounting described in SFAS 157. *Journal of Accounting and Public Policy* 27: 101–114.

Bienert, S. and Brunauer, W. (2007). The mortgage lending value: prospects for development within Europe. *Journal of Property Investment & Finance* 25 (6): 542–578.

Bohm, P. and Lind, H. (1993). Policy evaluation quality: a quasi-experimental study of regional employment subsidies in Sweden. *Regional Science and Urban Economics* 23 (1): 51–65.

Braun, N. (2016). Google search volume, sentiment and its impact on REIT market movements. *Journal of Property Investment & Finance* 34 (3): 249–262.

Braun, T. and Bienert, S. (2015). Is green (still) a matter of prime? stylized facts about the location of commercial green buildings. *Journal of Sustainable Real Estate* 7 (1): 160–182.

Bretten, J. and Wyatt, P. (2001). Variance in commercial property valuations for lending purposes: an empirical study. *Journal of Property Investment & Finance* 19 (3): 267–282.

Brooks, M. and McArthur, J.J. (2019). Drivers of investment in commercial real estate sustainability: 2006–2018. *Journal of Sustainable Real Estate* 11 (1): 130–155.

Burston, B. and Burrell, A. (2015). What is fair value? IPF Research Programme, Short Paper, p. 24.

Cole, R. and Eisenbeis, R. (1996). The role of principal-agent conflicts in the 1980's thrift crisis. *Journal of Real Estate Economics* 24 (2): 195–219.

Crosby, N. (2000). Valuation accuracy, variation and bias in the context of standards and expectations. *Journal of Property Investment & Finance* 18 (2): 130–161.

Crosby, N. and Hughes, C. (2011). The basis of valuations for secured commercial property lending in the UK. *Journal of European Real Estate Research* 4 (3): 225–242.

Crosby, N., French, N., and Oughton, M. (2000). Bank lending valuation on commercial property. Does European mortgage lending value add anything to the process? *Journal of Property Valuation and Investment* 18 (1): 36–49.

Crosby, N., Lizieri, C., and McAllister, P. (2010). Means, motive and opportunity? Disentangling client influence on performance measurement appraisals. *Journal of Property Research* 27 (2): 181–201.

Crosby, N., Devaney, S., and Wyatt, P. (2018). The implied rate of return in conventional valuation of development sites. *Journal of Property Research* 35 (3): 234–251.

d'Amato, M. (2018). Supporting property valuation with automatic reconciliation. *Journal of European Real Estate Research* 11 (1): 125–138.

d'Amato, M. and Kauko, T. (2017). *Advances in Automated Valuation Modelling: AVM After the Non-Agency Mortgage Crisis.* Springer Verlag.

Davis, J.M. and Wyndelts, R.W. (1979). Component depreciation for a shopping center. *The Appraisal Journal* 47 (2): 204–211.

Deaconu, A. and Buiga, A. (2010). Analysis of the convergence degree between the accounting and the valuation standards concerning fair value. *Journal of Property Investment & Finance* 28 (5): 365–384. https://doi.org/10.1108/14635781011069972.

DeLisle, J. Grissom, T. & Högberg, L. (2013), Sustainable real estate: an empirical study of the behavioural response of developers and investors to the LEED rating system. *Journal of Property Investment & Finance*, vol 31, No 1, pp. 10–40.

DeLisle, J.R., Never, B., and Grissom, T.V. (2020). The big data regime shift in real estate. *Journal of Property Investment & Finance* 38 (4): 363–395.

Diaz, J. (1999). The first decade of behavioral research in the discipline of property. *Journal of Property Investment & Finance* 17 (4): 326–332.

Diaz, J. III and Hansz, J.A. (2010). A taxonomic field investigation in to induced bias in residential real estate appraisals. *International Journal of Strategic Property Management* 14 (1): 3–17.

Ekelid, M., Lind, H., Lundström, S., and Persson, E. (1998). Treatment of uncertainty in appraisals of commercial properties: some evidence from Sweden. *Journal of Property Valuation & Investment* 16 (4): 386–396.

Fama, E. (2014). Two pillars of asset pricing. *American Economic Review* 104 (6): 1467–1485. http://dx.doi.org/10.1257/aer.104.6.1467.

French, N. (2001). Uncertainty in property valuation: the pricing of flexible leases. *Journal of Corporate Real Estate* 3 (1): 16–27.

French, N. (2012). The discounted cash flow method for property appraisals. *Journal of Property Investment & Finance* 30 (3): 325–329.

French, N. (2020). Property valuation in the UK: material uncertainty and COVID-19. *Journal of Property Investment & Finance* 38 (5): 463–470.

French, N. and Antill, J. (2018). Property valuation in the UK: energy efficiency legislation and its impact on valuation. *Journal of Property Investment & Finance* 36 (4): 383–390.

French, N. and Gabrielli, L. (2018). Property valuation revisited: the hierarchy of valuation approaches, methods and models. *Journal of Property Investment & Finance* 36 (4): 391–396.

French, N. and Sloane, N. (2018). Property valuation in the UK: implicit versus explicit models – the baby and the bathwater. *Journal of Property Investment & Finance* 36 (4): 397–406.

Friedman, M. (1953). The methodology of positive economics. In: *Essays in Positive Economics* (ed. M. Friedman), 3–43. Chicago, IL: University of Chicago Press.

Garber, P. (2000). Famous first bubbles. *Journal of Economic Perspectives* 4 (2): 35–54.

Geanakoplos, J.D. (2010). The leverage cycle. Cowles Foundation Discussion Paper No. 715R.

Geiger, P., Cajias, M., and Fuerst, F. (2016). A class of its own: the role of sustainable real estate in a multi-asset portfolio. *Journal of Sustainable Real Estate* 8 (1): 190–218.

Geltner, D., MacGregor, B., and Schwann, G. (2003). Appraisal smoothing and price discovery in real estate markets. *Urban Studies* 40 (5–6): 1047–1064.

Gilliland, C.E. (1980). Component depreciation – the appraiser's role. *The Appraisal Journal* 4 (1): 78–84.

Glaeser, E. (2013). A nation of gamblers: real estate speculation and American history. *American Economic Review: Papers & Proceedings* 103 (3): 1–42. http://dx.doi.org/10.1257/aer.103.3.1.

Goetzmann, W. and Peng, L. (2006). Estimating house price indexes in the presence of seller reservation prices. *The Review of Economics and Statistics* 88 (1): 100–112.

Grover, R. (2016). Mass valuations. *Journal of Property Investment & Finance* 34 (2): 191–204.

Guo, J., Chiang, S., Liu, M. et al. (2020). Can machine learning algorithms associated with text mining from internet data improve housing price prediction performance? *International Journal of Strategic Property Management* 24 (5): 300–312.

Gustafsson, C., Lind, H., and Lundström, S. (2019). *Fastighetsvärdering - då nu och i framtiden*. Stockholm: KTH Royal Institute of Technology, Instant Press.

Hansz, A. (2004). The use of a pending mortgage reference point in valuation judgment J. *Journal of Property Investment & Finance* 22 (3): 259–268.

Haurin, D. (2005). US commercial real estate indices: transaction-based and constant-liquidity indices. BIS Papers Chapters. In: *Real Estate Indicators and Financial Stability*, vol. 21 (ed. Bank for International Settlements), 232–242. Bank for International Settlements.

Havard, T. (2002). *Investment Property Valuation Today*. London, England: Estates Gazette.

Hayek, F.A. (1945). The use of knowledge in society. *The American Economic Review* 35 (4): 519–530.

Hill, S., Lorenz, D., Dent, P., and Lützkendorf, T. (2013). Professionalism and ethics in a changing economy. *Building Research & Information* 41 (1): 8–27.

Hirsch, J. and Hahn, J. (2018). How flood risk impacts residential rents and property prices: empirical analysis of a German property market. *Journal of Property Investment & Finance* 36 (1): 50–67.

Hirsch, J., Braun, B., and Bienert, S. (2015). Assessment of climatic risks for real estate. *Property Management* 33 (5): 494–518.

Hitz, J.-M. (2007). The decision usefulness of fair value accounting – a theoretical perspective. *European Accounting Review* 16 (2): 323–362.

Hoesli, M. and Oikarinen, E. (2012). *Are REITs Real Estate? Evidence from International Sector Level Data?* Research Papers series no. 12–15. Swiss Finance Institute.

Hordijk, A., Rompelman, D. and Koerhuis, L. (2010), Ten years of sale-and-leaseback transactions in The Netherlands: large-area office space contract rent some one-fifth above market rent, *Journal of Corporate Real Estate*, Vol. 12 No. 1, pp. 26–32. https://doi.org/10.1108/14630011011025898.

IAASB (2019). Overview of ISA 540 (revised) and conforming and consequential amendments to other standards, Slide show, International Auditing and Assurance Standards Board. https://www.slideshare.net/IFAC_Multimedia/isa-540-revised-overview (accesssed 10 January 2019).

IAM - Institute of Asset Management (2015). *Asset Management - An Anatomy*. Bristol, UK: IAM - Institute of Asset Management.

IAS 16 (2020). *Property, Plant & Equipment, IFRS – International Financial Reporting Standards, Consolidated Without Early Application*. London: International Accounting Standards Board.

IAS 40 (2020). *Investment Property, IFRS – International Financial Reporting Standards, Consolidated Without Early Application*. London: International Accounting Standards Board.

IFRS 13 (2020). *Fair Value Measurement, IFRS – International Financial Reporting Standards, Consolidated Without Early Application*. London: International Accounting Standards Board.

IFRS 3 (2020). *Business Combinations, IFRS – International Financial Reporting Standards, Consolidated Without Early Application*. London: International Accounting Standards Board.

IVSC, International Valuation Standards Council (2019). International Valuation Standards. London.

JLL (2018). Global real estate transparency index 2018. Transparency: Data, disclosure and disruption.

Joe, J.R., Vandervelde, S.D., and Wu, Y.-J. (2017). Use of high quantification evidence in fair value audits; do auditors stay in their comfort zone? *The Accounting Review* 92 (5): 89–119.

Kam, V. (1990). *Accounting Theory*. NY, USA: John Wiley & Sons Inc.

Kay, J. and King, M. (2020). *Radical Uncertainty – Decision Making for an Unknowable Future*. London, England: The Bridge Street Press.

King, M. (2016). *The End of Alchemy – Money, Banking, and the Future of the Global Economy*. New York, USA: W.W. Norton & Company, Inc.

Klamer, P., Bakker, C. and Gruis, V. (2017), Research bias in judgement bias studies – a systematic review of valuation judgement literature, *Journal of Property Research*, 2017 https://doi.org/10.1080/09599916.2017.1379552.

Klamer, P., Gruis, V., and Bakker, C. (2019). How client attachment affects information verification in commercial valuation practice. *Journal of Property Investment & Finance* https://doi.org/10.1108/JPIF-04-2019-0059.

Klemperer, P. (2004). *Auctions: Theory and Practice*. Princeton: Princeton University Press.

Knoll, K., Schularick, M., and Steger, T. (2017). No price like home: global house prices, 1870–2012. *American Economic Review* 107 (2): 331–353.

Kummerow, M. and Galfalvy, H. (2002). Error trade-offs in regression analysis appraisal methods. In: *Real Estate Valuation Theory* (eds. K. Wang and M. Wolverton), 105–131. Springer Verlag.

Levy, D. and Schuck, E. (1999). The influence of clients on valuations. *Journal of Property Investment & Finance* 17 (4): 380–400.

Levy, D. and Schuck, E. (2005). The influence of clients on valuations: the clients' perspective. *Journal of Property Investment & Finance* 23 (2): 182–201.

Lind, H. (1998). The definition of market value – criteria for judging proposed definitions and ananalysis of three controversial components. *Journal of Property Valuation & Investment* 16 (2): 159–174.

Lind, H. (2005). Value concepts, value information and cycles on the real estate market A comment on Crosby, French and Oughton (2000). *Journal of Property Investment & Finance* 23 (2): 141–147.

Lind, H. (2009). Price bubbles in housing markets: concept, theory and indicators. *International Journal of Housing Markets and Analysis* 2: 78–90.

Lind, H. and Lundström, S. (1996). Valuation of public real estate: context and concept. *Journal of Property Valuation and Investment* 14 (4): 31–40.

Lind, H. and Nordlund, B. (2014). A transparent two-step categorization of valuation methods. *The Appraisal Journal* 87: 244–250.

Lind, H. and Nordlund, B. (2019). The concept of market value in thin markets and its implications for international accounting rules (IFRS). *Journal of Property Investment & Finance* 37 (3): 301–310.

Lind, H. and Nyström, J. (2011). The explanation of incomplete contracts in mainstream contract theory: a critique of the distinction between "observable" and "verifiable". *Evolutionary and Institutional Economics Review* 7 (2): 279–293.

Lind, H. and Persson, E. (1998). The quest for a market related value concept that is not current market value. Working paper no. 31, Royal Institute of Technology, Stockholm.

Lorenz, D. and Lützkendorf, T. (2008). Sustainability in property valuation: theory and practice. *Journal of Property Investment & Finance* 26 (6): 482–521.

Lorenz, D. and Lützkendorf, T. (2011). Sustainability and property valuation: systematisation of existing approaches and recommendations for future action. *Journal of Property Investment Finance* 29 (6): 644–676.

Lorenz, D., Trück, S., and Lützkendorf, T. (2006). Addressing risk and uncertainty in property valuations: a viewpoint from Germany. *Journal of Property Investment & Finance* 24 (5): 400–433.

Lorenz, D., Dent, P., and Kauko, T. (2019). *Value in a Changing Built Environment.* Oxford: Wiley Blackwell.

Mäki, J. (2020), The role of investment property appraisal in European real estate companies, *Journal of European Real Estate Research*, Vol. 13 No. 1, pp. 105–122. https://doi.org/10.1108/JERER-11-2019-0038.

Małkowska, A., Uhruska, M., and Tomal, M. (2019). Age and experience versus susceptibility to client pressure among property valuation professionals— implications for rethinking institutional framework. *Sustainability* 11: 6759. https://doi.org/10.3390/su11236759.

Mallinson, M. (1994). *The Mallinson Report: Commercial Property Valuations.* London: The Royal Institute of Chartered Surveyors.

Mallinson, M. and French, N. (1999). Uncertainty in property valuation. The nature and relevance of uncertainty and how it might be measured and reported. *Journal of Property Investment & Finance* 18 (1): 13–32.

Mangioni, V. (2015). A review of the practices of valuers in the assessment of land value for taxation in Australia. *Journal of Property Tax Assessment & Administration* 12 (2): 5–15.

Martin, R.D., Rich, J.S., and Wilks, T.J. (2006). Auditing fair value measurements: a synthesis of relevant research. *Accounting Horizons* 20 (3): 287–303.

McAllister, P. (2020). Can brokers rig the real estate market? An exploratory study of the commercial real estate sector. *Journal of Property Research* 37 (3): 254–288. https://doi.org/10.1080/09599916.2020.1794935.

McParland, C., Adair, A., and McGreal, S. (2002). Valuation standards: a comparison of four European countries. *Journal of Property Investment & Finance* 20 (2): 127–141.

Meins, E. and Sager, D. (2015). Sustainability and risk: combining Monte Carlo simulation and DCF for swiss residential buildings. *Journal of European Real Estate Research* 8 (1): 66–84.

Miller, N., Gabe, J., and Sklarz, M. (2019). The impact of water front location on residential home values considering flood risks. *Journal of Sustainable Real Estate* 11 (1): 84–107.

Morri, G. and Benedetto, P. (2019). *Commercial Property Valuation.* Chichester: Wiley.

Nellessen, T. and Zuelch, H. (2011), The reliability of investment property fair values under IFRS, *Journal of Property Investment & Finance*, Vol. 29 No. 1, pp. 59–73, https://doi.org/10.1108/14635781111100209.

Nordlund, B. (2008). Valuation and performance reporting in property companies according to IFRS. Doctoral dissertation. KTH Royal Institute of Technology, Stockholm.

Nordlund, B. (2010). Need for disclosure regarding property valuations in financial reports according to IFRS. *Journal of Property Investment & Finance* 28 (5): 333–353. https://doi.org/10.1108/14635781011069954.

Nordlund, B. (2014). Property returns, free cash-flows and need for disclosures. *EPRA News*, No 47, pp 19–20, European Public Real Estate Association, Brussels, Belgium.

Nordlund, B., Lorentzon, J., and Lind, H. (2020). *Auditing Fair Value of Investment Properties – A Swedish Case Study*. Karlstad, Sweden: Karlstads universitet.

Nordlund, B., Lorentzon, J., and Lind, H. (2021). A note on auditing Fair Value of investment properties, *Journal of Property Investment and Finance*, available at https://www.emerald.com/insight/content/doi/10.1108/JPIF-01-2021-0009/full/html

Oyedokun, T., Dunse, N., and Jones, C. (2018). The impact of green premium on the development of green-labeled offices in the U.K. *Journal of Sustainable Real Estate* 10 (1): 81–108.

Oyewo, B., Emebinah, E., and Savage, R. (2020). Challenges in auditing fair value measurement and accounting estimates – some evidence from the field. *Journal of Financial Reporting and Accounting* 18 (1): 51–75.

Özdilek, U. (2012). An overview of the enquiries on the issue of apportionment of value between land and improvements. *Journal of Property Research* 29 (1): 69–84.

Özdilek, U. (2016). Property price separation between land and building components. *The Journal of Real Estate Research* 38 (2): 205–228.

Palm, P. and Andersson, M. (2020). Anchor effects in appraisals: do information and theoretical knowledge matter? *Journal of European Real Estate Research* https://doi.org/10.1108/JERER-03-2020-0012.

Penman, S.H. (2007). Financial reporting quality: is fair value a plus or a minus? *Accounting and Business Research* 37 (sup1): 33–44. https://doi.org/10.1080/00014788.2007.9730083.

Pomykacz, M. and Olmsted, C. (2013). Options in Real Estate Valuation. *The Appraisal Journal* 81 (3): 227–238.

PWC (2014). In depth – a look at current financial reporting issues: IFRS 13 European real estate Q9 survey, PWC. inform.pwc.com.

Quan, D. and Quigley, J. (1991). Price formation and the appraisal function in real estate markets. *Journal of Real Estate Finance and Economics* 4: 127–146.

Ratcliff, R. (1972). *Valuation for Real Estate Decisions*. Santa Cruz: Democrat Press.

Reid, B. (2016). *Private Real Estate: Valuation and Sale Price Comparison*. MSCI.

Reid, B. (2019), *Real Estate May Be Yielding Less Than You Thought*, MSCI, New York, NY available at https://www.msci.com/www/blog-posts/real-estate-may-be-yielding/01591066353.

RICS (2012). *Sustainability and commercial property valuation*. RICS guidance note, global. London, England: The Royal Institution of Chartered Surveyors (RICS).

RICS (2017). *The Future of Valuations - The Relevance of Real Estate Valuations for Institutional Investors and Banks –Views from a European Expert Group*. London, England: The Royal Institution of Chartered Surveyors (RICS).

RICS (2018). *Bank Lending Valuations and Mortgage Lending Value*, 1e, RICS professional standards and guidance, Europe. London, England: Royal Institution of Chartered Surveyors (RICS).

RICS (2019). *RICS valuation – global standards. RICS professional standards and guidance, global.* London, England: The Royal Institution of Chartered Surveyors (RICS).

Robinson, S. and McAllister, P. (2015). Heterogeneous price premiums in sustainable real estate? An investigation of the relation between value and price premiums. *Journal of Sustainable Real Estate* 7 (1): 1–20.

Robinson, S. and Singh, A.J. (2019). The impact of green labels on U.S. hotel net operating income: operating statements analyses. *Journal of Sustainable Real Estate* 11 (1): 156–173.

Runde, T.R. and Thoyre, S. (2010). Integrating sustainability and green building in to the appraisal process. *Journal of Sustainable Real Estate* 2 (1): 221–248.

Rushmore, S. (1992). *Hotels and Motels: A Guide to Market Analysis, Investment Analysis and Valuation.* Chicago: Appraisal Institute.

Saduyaki, T., Harano, K., and Yamazaki, F. (2019). Market transparency and international real estate investment. *Journal of Property Investment & Finance* 37 (5): 503–518.

Salzman, D.A. and Zwinkels, R. (2017). Behavioural real estate. *Journal of Real Estate Literature* 25 (1): 77–106.

Scarrett, D. and Osborn, S. (2014). *Property Valuation: The Five Methods*, 3e. Routledge.

Sebastian, S. and Schätz, A. (2009). *Real Estate Equities—Real Estate or Equities?* IRE BS International Real Estate Business School.

Selling, T.I. and Nordlund, B. (2015). The problem of management bias in accounting estimates: an investor perspective on root causes and solutions. *Business Horizons* 58 (5): 501–508.

Shiller, R.J. (2000). *Irrational Exuberance.* Princeton, NJ: Princeton University Press.

Shiller, R.J. (2014). Speculative asset prices. *American Economic Review* 104 (6): 1486–1517.

Song, H.-S. and Wilhelmsson, M. (2010). Improved price index for condominiums. *Journal of Property Research* 27 (1): 39–60.

Stiglitz, J. (1990). Symposium on bubbles. *Journal of Economic Perspectives* 4: 13–18.

Tajani, F. and Morano, P. (2018). An empirical-deductive model for the assessment of the mortgage lending value of properties as securities for credit exposures. *Journal of European Real Estate Research* 11 (1): 44–70.

Tajani, F., Morano, P., Salvo, F., and Ruggiero, M. (2020). Property valuation: the market approach optimised by a weighted appraisal model. *Journal of Property Investment & Finance* 38 (5): 399–418.

Thorne, C. (2009). Value: fair or foul. *EPRA News* (March), pp. 14–17.

Valier, A. (2020). Who performs better? AVMs vs hedonic models. *Journal of Property Investment & Finance* 38 (3): 213–225.

Vimpari, J. (2018). Pricing lease agreements incorporating tenant's downscaling option. *Journal of European Real Estate Research* 11 (3): 427–439.

Vimpari, J. and Junnila, S. (2014). Valuing green building certificates as real options. *Journal of European Real Estate Research* 7 (2): 181–198.

Walvekar, G. and Kakka, V. (2020). Private Real Estate: Valuation and Sale Price Comparison 2019. MSCI, Research Report, June 2020.

Wyatt, P. (2009). Replacement cost and market Value. *Journal of Property Investment & Finance* 27 (6): 593–602.

Wyatt, P. (2013). *Property Valuation*, 2e. Oxford: Wiley-Blackwell.

Young, M.S., Fisher, J.D., and D'Alessandro, J. (2017). New NCREIF value index and operations measures. *Journal of Real Estate Literature* 25 (1): 221–235.

Zalejska-Jonsson, A., Lind, H., and Hintze, S. (2012). Low-energy versus conventional residential buildings: cost and profit. *Journal of European Real Estate Research* 5 (3): 211–228.

Index

Advanced Issues in Property Valuation, First Edition. Hans Lind and Bo Nordlund.
© 2021 John Wiley & Sons Ltd. Published 2021 by John Wiley & Sons Ltd.